A Positive Workplace
Means Business!
It Just Makes Cent$! ™

Copyrighted Material

Dedication

I dedicate this book to my wonderful sons,
Timothy and Daniel Paris.

The world is a better place because of the fine men
you have become.
It has been my privilege and blessing
to be your Mom.
I love you and am so very proud of you.

Table of Contents

About the Author

Mary Jane Paris, aka "MJ" as she is know by her friends and colleagues, is the President of Positive Impact Consulting Services, LLC, in Shelton, CT, a company she founded in 2006. She has a proven track record of delivering results and brings to her practice a broad base of experience gained from more than 25 years in management, sales, retail banking, training, recruiting, coaching, project management, event planning and community leadership.

Her common sense approach and practical experience combined with her dynamic presentation skills provide a solid foundation for understanding her client's needs and challenges.

MJ is a recognized leader in the academic and business communities and is a tireless volunteer and fundraiser for many organizations in her area.

Along with her consulting practice, she is an Adjunct Professor in the Business Administration Department at Housatonic Community College, Bridgeport, CT. MJ is a member of the Society for Human Resource Management (SHRM), the American Society for Training and Development (ASTD), and is a National Speakers Association (NSA) associate.

For more information, visit the author's website at www.posimpact.net.

Acknowledgements

This book has been my "dream in the works" for many years. It would not have been possible without the encouragement and support of many people - family, friends, and colleagues - over the years.

To my parents, Jane and Carl, for the unconditional love they gave and what they taught me about real success in life by the way they lived.

To my sons, Tim and Dan, their spouses, Amy and Katy, for their spirit, understanding, patience and encouragement to live my dreams.

To my "little people," my granddaughters, Isabelle and Gabrielle, for teaching me about genuine people-to-people connections, imagination, creativity, and having fun!

To my dear Aunt Rose and Uncle Jim DeGaro, for always being there for me and taking the time to share their gifts with me.

To my BFF, Rosemary Andreana Occhino, for giving me over 60 years of friendship and for sharing her beloved, Joe, one of the "good guys" and a jewel in the crown of life, who left us too soon.

To the "NaNa's" (Cathy Salatino and Donna Fraley), my Gloversville girlfriends, for our history and journey of so many wonderful years.

To Helen Bassett, who, through her warm, adventurous spirit and globe trotting, brought a "world of friendship" to me.

I am grateful to those who entered my life as professors, advisors, managers, and mentors and became friends…for believing in me, listening to me, sharing with me, connecting me, and for bringing out the best in me over the years, especially Joyce Budd, Mike Del Re Jr., Joan Gallagher, Nancie Gray, Ed Hendricks, Barbara Johnson, Lillie Margaret Lazaruk, Carol Pluchino, and Nancy Sidoti.

I am grateful to the "Positive Workplace" leaders and role models who granted me interviews for this book – Cindy Bigelow, Patrick Charmel, Larry Janesky, Robert Scinto and Jill Leonard Tavello. Learning about their history, their dreams, their persistence, their courage and faith gave me inspiration to go for it!

In addition, I would like to acknowledge those professionals who literally make me "look good" – my stylist, Paula Szarmach, P.J. & Company Salon, Shelton, CT; Fred Ortoli, Fred Ortoli Photography, Oxford, CT; Von Lee, Graphic Designer, Fairfield, CT, Malin Zergiebel, Carolyn Moore, Leslie Huston, TSG WebPlus, Brookfield, CT.

And, to all the rest…those people along the way that I have met, taught, worked with, worked for, provided service to, received service from, simply smiled at, travelled with, and casually brushed by in passing…the journey would not have been the same without you!

Introduction

A Positive Workplace Means Business! It Just Makes "Cent$!" ™

That's my platform…That's my mantra! When we think and talk about a "Positive Workplace," we need to begin with each of us, as individuals, and the fact that we come to work each day as "people" – *first!* Complete with our experience, skills, and most importantly, our attitudes, we step over the threshold each day and become employees.

We make choices each day – what we wear, what we eat, what we do, what we say to ourselves. One of the big choices is what attitude we bring to work each day – it's either a positive or negative! This choice of attitude affects our self-talk and our thoughts; our thoughts affect our behavior and our actions – either positively or negatively.

Whichever the case, these very attitudes influence our choices, interactions, our work, our peers, colleagues, vendors, and the overall workplace environment. Our attitudes about our differences and our actions that either include or exclude – are critical in this process.

Fair and consistent treatment of employees is a must in the workplace. Managers put themselves and their organizations at risk when they treat employees unprofessionally or illegally.

A colleague of mine once used a wonderful phrase, he said… *"A company doesn't own your soul, but they rent your behavior!"*

No matter what the industry or business sector, "Positive Workplaces" are built on successful people-to-people ("P2P") relationships, positive interactions and behavior, beginning with the most critical component, the partnership between managers and employees. This relationship sets the tone and impacts the workplace.

The workplace environment drives employees! Employees drive your business!

The message is a simple one yet, difficult for organizations to implement and manage.

Working brings us into close and frequent contact with others. The physical environment of many workplaces – especially those with workstations and cubicles – leaves little room for employees to experience quiet, distraction-free or private surroundings.

Given the close proximity of people in the workplace, technology and its affect on our time, the global business culture, and the on-going social and networking interactions, we live in a hectic, fast-paced business world! We can easily forget about the importance of the developing and maintaining the people-to-people connections.

It doesn't matter whether we are self-employed, or work for a small business, not-for-profit, educational institution or large corporation, we all need to remember the basics and keep it simple to survive and thrive in the 21st century.

Research has proven what we already know – that negative, toxic environments disengage and de-motivate employees, while positive, supportive environments engage and motivate our most valuable asset.

We also know that no workplace will ever be perfect – since we, the people working there, are not perfect! We can, however, do our best to make it as positive as possible – one person at a time, one day at a time – to engage ourselves, our employees, our customers and improve our business results.

This book was created from lots of research, as noted in the "Resources and References" section in the back of the book. It is a collection of various nuggets of knowledge about what I believe, what I've learned from reading and, most importantly, from the people-to-people ("P2P") connections that have made a positive impact on my life and career journey. A business associate recently described me as a "share-it-all" and I'd like to share some of my findings with you.

It is my hope that each chapter of this book will help you to open your mind, improve your attitude, heighten your personal awareness and change disengaging behavior to create a more positive workplace for yourself and your colleagues.

As you read each page, remember…

A Positive Workplace
Means Business!
It Just Makes Cent$! TM

"Turn Up Your Dimmer Switch!"

Make a positive impact on your personal life, your career and bottom-line results!

Thank you for joining me on this journey…

Chapter One

Power-Up! It's All About You!

Nowhere do we need "positive energy" more than in the workplace. We all know people who possess it, and usually we look forward to their contributions and interacting with them. Whether senior managers or front line workers, they have gained the deep respect and admiration of most of the workforce.

So, Power-Up! Take a look at some basic tips toward becoming such a person yourself.

Top 10 Ways to Become Someone YOU Would Respect & Admire at Work

10. Never lie. Period!
9. Really listen to people, paraphrasing what you think you hear to check understanding.
8. Accept responsibility for all of your feelings. No one "makes me feel" anything.
7. Don't talk about people behind their backs. What goes around comes around.
6. Don't spread rumors, if you can avoid it. Check it out at the source first.
5. Refrain from, or respectfully confront, disrespectful and inappropriate jokes, gossip, plots and conspiracies. There is almost always someone nearby who will appreciate it.
4. Catch people being nice, and/or doing good work, and call them on it.

3. If wronged, avoid the temptation to seek revenge. It hurts you more than it hurts them.
2. Don't hold grudges. They don't look good on you.

Number 1. **Accept responsibility for your words and actions, especially your mistakes. Personal power means never *fearing* to say you're sorry.**

A Positive Workplace
Means Business!
It Just Makes Cent$! ᴛᴍ

Chapter Two

What Business Are You Really In?

As we begin to explore the importance of a *Positive Workplace*, I'd like you to think about the answers to these three questions…

1. **What business are you in?**
2. **What really drives your employees?**
3. **Who is really driving your business?**

Did you answer questions #1 with the product or service you provide? Did you answer question #2 with the word "money?" Did you answer question #3 with either your name or those of your upper management? If you did, you are not alone!

In today's global workplace, many employees are being stretched to the max! (You may be one of them.) They are doing more with less, leaving them feeling stressed, overwhelmed and disengaged – burned out – leading to lower productivity, internal/external customer service issues, and turnover, all of which impacts bottom-line results.

Did you know it costs about 250% of salary (recruiting, training, operational issues) each time an employee turns over?

I work with many "for-profit" and "not-for-profit" businesses/organizations who understand that we are *all* in the *"people"* business and how important it is to strengthen the skills of those who are really running their business – *the employees.*

The partnership between managers and employees has a great impact on the workplace environment. When the manager/supervisor's attitude sets a negative tone and creates an environment that is negative and toxic, employees tend to be negative, feel under-developed, disengaged, de-motivated, unproductive, and deliver poor customer service. Employee morale is low, turnover is high and business results suffer!

When the attitude, tone and environment are positive and supportive, employees tend to be more positive, feel they are being developed, are engaged, productive, motivated and deliver WOW customer service! Employee morale is high, turnover is low! Think about what happens when customers come to us looking for solutions to issues or problems they are facing and WOW service is delivered! They return, refer others and, voila! Personal, professional, and business results improve!

As a manager/supervisor, what is the single most important thing you want your employees to do each day to improve your business? *Come to work!*

As an employee, what is the single most important thing you can do to advance your career and job performance? *Come to work!*

So, doesn't it make sense that we, the people at all levels of organizations, understand that the workplace environment really drives employees? Isn't it commonsensical that we understand the role we play and really see the connection between the workplace environment and business results?

No matter what the industry or business sector, "Positive Workplaces" are built on successful "people-to-people" ("P2P") relationships. The message is a simple one yet, difficult for organizations to implement and manage.

Leaders of the 21st century are being continually challenged with improving performance, profitability and market share and are responsible for developing their organization's people and customer service strategies.

What's the People-to-People ("P2P") Connection?

Employees (the people) at all levels are an organization's largest asset and highest expense. Front-line employees are the key to successfully executing their organization's customer service strategies. They need to better understand their role in building relationships with internal and external customers and how their people-to-people ("P2P") relationships drive business results.

The workplace environment drives employees!
Employees drive your business!

The top levels of any organization set the tone with ethical codes, standards, visions, goals, and most importantly, with their behavior. How can we ask employees to behave or perform in an expected way when those who are leading the organization are not setting the standard and living the model?

We – the managers and employees – create a positive or negative workplace environment through our own *attitudes and interactions* with each other. What happens within these primary relationships are the basis for either success or failure – for individual careers, work groups, departments, divisions and, overall, results of the organization.

Sounds simple, right? It's easier said than done! The journey is on-going! The need for leadership and professional development is a continuous process and critical to attracting and retaining the best talent, reducing turnover, improving engagement, productivity, service and achieving bottom-line results in all organizations.

The road to results is through the employees – the "P2P" connections - that's all of us!

A Positive Workplace
Means Business!
It Just Makes Cent$! ™

Chapter Three

It All Starts with Attitude!

Did you know that 75% of employees are unhappy in their current job?

Do you sometimes feel like you're in a slump and wish you had the tools to "snap out of it"?

Are you surrounded by co-workers, friends, family who are bringing you down and you don't know how to lift them up?

Have you ever thought about how your ***attitude*** affects…
- Personality and work performance?
- Your employees, your customers, your relationships and your work environment?
- Workforce diversity, career success, and teamwork?
- Bottom-line results?

It All Starts with Attitude!

It All Starts with…"Positive *Self-Talk*"

We – the managers and employees – create a positive or negative workplace environment through our own *attitudes and actions* with each other.

We are first, "individuals" in the workplace. When we come through the door each day, we bring with us our attitudes, global views, beliefs, experiences and knowledge – which have a combined affect on our behavior. Some of us come with difficult and challenging personal lives which, unfortunately, affect our behavior and attitudes on the job.

Let's take the First Step…. It all starts with **attitude!** Attitudes are the *foundation* – one person at a time – for creating a Positive Workplace!

A positive attitude is a priceless possession for personal fulfillment and career success. It is also an essential element for creating a positive workplace.

When I think about the basics elements of human relationships, I think primarily about the attitude we each bring to relationships, whether they are personal or professional in nature. What is the first thing you remember about someone you meet? Chances are it's their attitude!

We all know what a positive attitude sounds like, but how can we define it?

Simply stated, noted authors, Chapman and McKnight, describe it as the way you look at things mentally, your *mental focus* on the world. It's never static; it's always in flux – the result of an on-going process that's dynamic and sensitive to what's going on.

Events, circumstances, and messages – both positive and negative – can affect your attitude. A positive attitude can be infectious!

Business is complex and competitive – with comparable resources, including people. Chapman and McKnight say, "People with a positive attitude are looking up and forward and are more likely to work to higher standards of quality, safety, and productivity – individually and as a team. Working near a person with a positive attitude is an energizing experience; he/she can change the tone and morale of the department and make others feel more upbeat. Sometimes the reason people lack a positive attitude is simply that they don't realize that they have a negative one!" I agree…

A positive workplace is about the *people* and their *positive outlook* about their work and the organization that make the organization thrive. The war for talent exists. Do we want to hire and retain people with positive or negative attitudes? The answer is obvious… Hire for attitude; the mechanics of the job can be taught. A company gets its edge from the attitude of its people – its leaders, its supervisors, front-line, back-office, entry-level and long-term employees. The "P2P" connections…

Building and maintaining healthy, effective relationships in all directions – with people you work for, people you work with, and people who work for you – is a key to success. Unlike some other sports, business is a team sport. Nothing contributes more to the process of building effective work relationships than a positive attitude. More business successes are won on attitude than technical achievement. A supervisor who knows how to build a positive attitude can lead a departmental workforce with only average experience and skills to achieve high productivity and successful performance. It's called "teamwork" and it happens often!

It's important to remember that we all have a choice – to be either positive or negative in any situation – and we make those choices every day. By keeping our power and being aware of our own attitude and choices, we can protect ourselves from external circumstances and people's negativity. Safeguard your attitude by solving personal conflicts quickly, taking the "high road" if someone behaves unreasonably or unfairly, insulating or distancing yourself from a person with whom you have a repeated conflict, focusing on the work and changing your traffic pattern to avoid people who pull your attitude down.

Remember: Your attitude belongs to *you* and you alone!

What's the bottom-line? Nowhere is your positive attitude more appreciated by others than when you are at work. Being open to change and new ideas makes for positive changes and improved financial results. The business world consists of many people who are different from you. We're dependent on each other to achieve common goals. We need to understand and work effectively with all the labor resources. Opportunities for us to learn about other backgrounds, cultures broaden our perspective with new ideas, talents, and points of view – it all affects bottom-line results.

A word of caution – don't go overboard by becoming a noisy cheerleader who spends more effort on projecting your attitude than nurturing it. Above all, be *authentic*. Ah, my favorite word... Project the real thing!

Life is a learning journey and all we can do is to strive to do our best each day. A wise person once said, "If you place more emphasis on keeping a positive attitude than on making money, you'll be successful and the money will take care of itself."

Let's face it… no one can be positive all of the time! What we do know is that a positive attitude makes problem solving easier and the more you expect from a situation, the more success you will achieve (The High Expectancy Success Theory).

It All Starts with Attitude!
Is it time to tune-up your "Attitude Barometer?"

Take the first step on the road to tuning up your attitude with a check of your "Attitude Barometer." Be good to yourself, enjoy the ride and make a *Positive Impact* on your career, workplace, and organizational results with a positive attitude!

A Positive Workplace
Means Business!
It Just Makes Cent$! ™

Chapter Four

The Equation for Success

When you attend any of my programs, you will hear me ask, "How many of you liked algebra when you were in school?" With wonder, some participants eagerly raise their hands, while others groan at the thought, thinking, "What does algebra have to do with our business and our workplace?" You may be thinking the same thing…

Over the years, I've developed this simple equation that, in my opinion, represents the "Equation for Success" that works for all types of organizations.

$$EM + E2 + EC = PO + PW \text{ }_{TM}$$

Think you know how it translates? Read on…The partnership between managers and employees has a great impact on the workplace environment. When the manager/supervisor's attitude sets a negative tone and creates an environment that is negative and toxic, employees tend to be negative, feel under-developed, disengaged, de-motivated, unproductive, and deliver poor customer service. Employee morale is low, turnover is high and business results suffer!

It's all about *employee performance* – from the top down – driving business results! It just makes cent$!

Let's take a closer look…how would you answer these questions?

- What is your *organization's* performance standard?
- What is your *personal* performance standard?
- How would your *(internal and external) customers* rate your personal and organizational performance?
- How is the *environment* impacting you and your employees?
- If you are a *"people manager,"* how does your personal performance standard affect your employees and, ultimately, the *results* of the organization?

Research has proven…Leaders of successful, profitable organizations understand that reducing turnover and improving results begins with taking a good, hard look at where "the rubber meets the road" – at the people who are managing/supervising their employees.

They are asking some difficult questions of themselves and of those that report to them:
- Who's managing/supervising the day-to-day operations?
- Is this the right person for the job *today*?
- What is the turnover in their area?
- What is the workplace environment like in their area?
- What are the managers/supervisors doing or not doing to help their employees improve productivity and business results?
- How is employee performance managed? Is 99% good enough?
- How are employees trained either formally or on-the-job by managers/supervisors to perform their jobs effectively?

- How effective are the current employee training and development programs?

So, have you figured out how to translate the equation? It's all about the ("P2P") people-to-people connections that are really driving results...

EM *(Effective Managers)* + **E2** *(Engaged Employees)* + **EC** *(Engaged Customers)* =
PO *(Profitable Organization)* + **PW** *(Positive Workplace)*

A Positive Workplace
Means Business!
It Just Makes Cent$! ™

Chapter Five

Is 99% Good Enough?

You may remember the "quality" initiatives of the 1980's and '90's. At the turn of the new millennium (remember Y2K?), we heard about "continuous improvement efforts" in organizations. Today, the latest buzzwords, "performance excellence," are being used.

Whatever words you choose to use, it's always about measuring the standard of service/product output. What's your organization's standard? Reality says that "quality" standards of 100 percent are never going to be attained. After all, nobody's perfect. Wouldn't life be a whole lot easier and less stressful if we accepted a certain amount of predictable human error and build it into the margin? We could even call it something impressive and positive-sounding, like "acceptable quality level" or "the best we can do standard," for example.

As too many American businesses – "for-profit" and "not-for-profit" – have learned, the idea of an "acceptable" level of mistakes, errors, waste, spoilage – and, consequently, a corresponding level of disgruntled customers – is a trap that can lure an otherwise well-meaning company into the kind of organizational quicksand where size and strength can become a liability instead of an advantage.

In today's global economy, those who have been charting a course back to competitive excellence say the only acceptable quality level is 100 percent. That's the standard of measurement. The rationale is simple: Set a standard at 95 percent and people figure they're doing fine as long as they're at or near it. In the language of the Malcolm Baldridge National Quality Award, however, performance excellence (quality) is a "race with no finish line." There's no time of day or month on the calendar when it's okay to let up.

Think of it this way, the alternative to setting standards at their highest possible level becomes clearer when you look at the consequences of "almost but not quite." According to an article written by Natalie Gabel for Training Magazine a few years ago, if 99.9 percent is good enough then...

- Two million documents will be lost by the IRS this year
- 811,000 faulty rolls of 35mm film will be loaded this year
- 32,000 checks will be deducted from the wrong bank accounts in the next 60 minutes
- 1,314 phone calls will be misplaced by telecommunications services every minute
- 12 babies will be given to the wrong parents each day
- 268,500 defective tires will be shipped this year
- 14, 208 defective personal computers will be shipped this year
- 2,200 gallons of coffee assumed to be caffeinated will turn out to be decaf instead – but consumed nonetheless in just one tax firm during the tax season
- 103,260 income tax returns will be processed incorrectly this year
- 2,488,300 books will be shipped in the next 12 months with the wrong cover
- 5,517,200 cases of soft drinks produced in the next 12 months will be flatter than a bad tire

- Two plane landings daily at O'Hare International Airport in Chicago will be unsafe
- 3,056 copies of tomorrow's Wall Street Journal will be missing one of the three sections
- 18,322 pieces of mail will be mishandled in the next hour
- 291 pacemaker operations will be performed incorrectly this year
- 880,000 credit cards in circulation will turn out to have incorrect cardholder information on their magnetic strips
- $9,690 will be spent today, tomorrow, next Thursday and every day in the future on defective, often unsafe sporting equipment
- 55 malfunctioning ATM's will be installed in the next 12 months
- 20,000 incorrect drug prescriptions will be written in the next 12 months
- 114,500 mismatched pairs of shoes will be shipped this year
- $761,900 will be spend in the next 12 months on CD's and DVD's that won't play
- 107 incorrect medical procedures will be performed by the end of the day today
- 315 entries in the most recent Webster's New International Dictionary of the English Language (unabridged) will turn out to be misspelled

Incidentally, 99.9 percent accuracy would be a remarkable improvement in the context of current performance levels. For example:

- A Hewlett Packard study of 300,000 semiconductors from three American firms and three Japanese firms recently found the average failure rate of American chips was over 0.1

percent; the failure rate for Japanese-made chips was zero.

- Since 1995, according to the U.S. Bureau of Transportation, the U.S. airline industry, despite reams of advertising about improved performance, reported:

    o On-Time Arrivals: range from 73.23% - 81.59%
    o Late Departures: range from 16.25% - 20.06%
    o The airline industry also assumes five to ten percent of all luggage will be mishandled and three percent of all checked baggage will be lost en route.

- And don't look to the heavens for salvation: The Office of Technology Assessment recently published a report stating, "Of the more than 20,000 objects fired into orbit since 1957, fewer than five percent remain operational."

Again, I ask you...
- What about *your* workplace?
- What is your *organization's* performance standard? What is your *personal* performance standard?
- How would your *(internal and external) customers* rate your personal and organizational performance?
- How is the *environment* impacting you and your employees?
- If you are a *"people manager,"* how does your personal performance standard affect your employees and, ultimately, the *results* of the organization?

Is 99.9 percent good enough?

A Positive Workplace
Means Business!
It Just Makes Cent$! ™

Chapter Six

Fostering a Diverse and Inclusive Workplace

Leaders of 21st century organizations must manage diversity and practice inclusion well in order to make the Positive Impact on their organization's performance, profitability and market share.

We hear so much about "diversity" these days. In many organizations, much attention and effort has been given to promote diversity by increasing the representation of people of color, women and other groups in the workforce. However, by just increasing the numbers represented of any population is not enough to make a real difference in individual or organizational performance.

Employees at all levels must become more aware and learn about diversity and inclusion. It's so much more than the differences we can see!

A major change had taken place in recent years in the workforce: the cultural and generational mix of employees has become more diversified. The performance standards are the same, but the workforce mix is different. Our attitude and how we behave as managers and employees in this mix will make or break the environment, careers and business results.

Creating a more inclusive workplace and customer-friendly environment that capitalizes on the experiences and differences of others leads to increased productivity, higher levels of employee engagement, superior customer service, and improved overall business results.

To most people "diversity" means those differences that we can see. It's much more...It's also about what we *can't* see – disabilities, different experiences, personality styles, lifestyle choices, styles and perspectives. Diversity exists in just about every organization; differences, however, are seldom understood and rarely regarded or used as an asset.

Disability as a diversity component is receiving more and more focus. Did you know that people with disabilities make up $3 trillion in market share? (Yes, that's trillion!) People like to purchase from people like them or who include people like them - the 101 of the sales and marketing process. It's not only the right thing to do, it just makes cent$!

The issue becomes more about just *having* diversity (those things that make us different) in an organization. It's about understanding the true meaning of diversity and its powerful impact (both positive and negative) on individual and organizational performance.

How do you define "diversity?" Here's the definition I use: Diversity is about our global view or, simply stated, how we see the world on three levels. Ask yourself these three questions to determine your global view:

(1) Who am I? (things we cannot change – race, gender, ethnicity, age, sexual preference, differing abilities (physical/mental), etc.)

(2) What do I choose? (religion, education, family lifestyle, physical appearance, language, etc.)

(3) How am I in the workplace? (title, corporate employee, self-employed, cube dweller, posh office, manager, non-manager, etc.)

These three levels affect our thoughts, behaviors and outcomes of any given situation. They impact how we behave and act as individuals at home, at work or at play.

Few organizations devote much effort to enabling new or existing employees to feel included in the life of the organization. Surveys indicate that very few people feel welcome or able to contribute their full range of skills, experiences, ideas and opinions. Most feel they are expected to think, act and express themselves in conformance with a fairly narrow range of behaviors. As a result, few people fully invest the bulk of their energy to their job or the organization.

Changing an organization's work culture is not something that can be accomplished through a new mission statement, employee handbook, recruitment policy or mentoring program. It requires new ways of thinking about and working with people, both as individuals, in teams, inside, outside and at all levels of the organization. It's about creating a *positive workplace* environment where our differences and our similarities are fully appreciated and utilized. It's about creating and sustaining an *inclusive* workplace environment where:

- People feel a sense of belonging
- People feel respected, valued and SEEN for who they are

- There is a level of supportive energy and commitment from leaders, peers, and others so that _all_ people can do their best work

Having "diversity" without "inclusion" is not enough. What then is the true meaning of diversity? Simply stated,

Diversity = _Differences._ Inclusion = _Action._

And _action_ is the key word! Every day, we can each contribute to a more inclusive workplace environment through our own individual actions by becoming more aware of our implicit biases, attitudes and behaviors in every situation or interaction. More importantly, we need to recognize and _respond_ to situations where co-workers and customers do not feel included.

Inclusive workplace environments that leverage diversity and practice inclusion have seen measurable, positive change, such as increased productivity, improved customer service and reduced turnover. The leaders of 21st century organizations must manage diversity and practice inclusion well in order to make the _Positive Impact_ on their organization's performance, profitability and market share.

You can start first thing tomorrow morning by greeting everyone you see and calling those you know by name. It all starts with a simple "hello."

*A Positive Workplace
Means Business!
It Just Makes Cent$!* TM

34

Chapter Seven

Effective Managers & Engaged Employees Driving Results

Let's take a closer look at the all-important partnership and key to creating a positive workplace and improved business results...the "P2P" partnership between managers and employees.

Every manager's contribution to the organization's mission and strategic goals has a direct correlation on their ability to retain and engage talented, highly skilled, knowledgeable people as employees.

Employees want to feel valued, empowered and appreciated and will most likely be more engaged and stay with an organization, as a result. The higher the engagement levels, the more their attitude barometer rises. The higher the attitude barometer rises, the more business results improve.

The irony of it all is that a work environment that is largely positive makes even the unpleasant tasks of managing employee performance and discipline more effective!

There are many ways in which managers and supervisors can create positive workplaces. To begin, they must define what a positive workplace is by "walking the walk" and "talking the talk" – by being authentic in establishing good relationships, improving teamwork and fostering innovations.

What are some of the manager's behaviors that have the most impact on employee engagement? Here's what Towers Perrin found in their research:

Manager Behaviors Having the Most Impact on Employee Engagement

1) *Supporting teamwork*
2) *Acting with honesty & integrity*
3) *Encouraging/empowering people to take initiative*
4) *Having valuable experience/expertise*
5) *Encouraging new ideas & new ways of doing things*
6) *Providing clear goals & direction*
7) *Inspiring enthusiasm for work*
8) *Ensuring access to a variety of learning opportunities*
9) *Helping employees understand how they impact financial performance*
10) *Building teams with diverse skills and backgrounds*

What about the employee side of the equation? What did the Towers Perrin research deem as the top drivers of employee engagement?

What Are The Top Drivers of Engagement From the Employee's Perspective? (In Order of Importance)

1) *Senior management's interest in employees' well-being*
2) *Challenging work*
3) *Decision-making authority*
4) *Evidence that the company is focused on customers*
5) *Career advancement opportunities*
6) *The company's reputation as a good employer*

7) *A collaborative work environment where people work well in teams*
8) *Resources to get the job done*
9) *Input on decision-making*
10) *A clear vision from senior management about future success*

Creating a "positive workplace" doesn't happen in a vacuum. It is important for managers to listen and communicate sincerely with their employees and provide positive reinforcement. According to Terry White, TheFabricator.com, there are three ways to develop this sincere relationship – balance, timing and clarity.

"Balance means having set standards for reinforcing actions. Timing means recognizing actions or achievements when they occur. Clarity means keeping praise simple and specific."

Today's managers are expected to build a work environment in which their key employees thrive, constantly learn and want to give their "all" to the organization. Effective, talent-minded managers know that if their organization is to be productive and competitive, they must not only "hang on" to good people, but also continually develop them in order to meet constantly changing business needs.

The Conference Board states: "Finding and keeping talent are critical elements of an organization's ability to improve profitability, manage costs, grow by acquisition, innovate, develop new products and services, and uncover new markets."

Engagement, Development and Self-Empowerment

Internal and external workshops and corporate education programs are all critical in the employee development process and have a positive impact on employee engagement. When employees feel they are empowered and are being developed, they become more engaged and productive.

If you wonder what your employees think about their career development – JUST ASK! Many organizations use surveys and measurement tools as the backbone of their career development strategy.

Other organizations have minimal career development activities in place and need to build a career development strategy from scratch. Leaders can be taught how to conduct career development discussions, formulate concepts, and assess educational opportunities that will drive the development process.

According to the Conference Board, the world's leading business membership organization, "…using a measurement tool, makes it easy to see the positive impact of the activities and communicate the success of the efforts from an unbiased perspective."

Self-esteem and personal success will increase by understanding the need for self-empowerment. Positive self-talk techniques give you new personal power!
- Improve your interpersonal and management skills
- Resolve conflict and defuse emotional reactions more positively

- Devise your own development plan to help you get what you want from life!

Positive attitude, self-talk and the feeling of empowerment lead to personal success and play a major role in professional success if you are willing to be honest with yourself and do the work!

One way or the other, employees drive your business! Either forward to improved profitability or backward into the ground! Who's really driving your business? What's it all about? It's about human relationships – the people-to-people ("P2P") connections – and the Equation for Success!

$$EM + E2 + EC = PO + PW \text{ }_{TM}$$

The foundation is set with an *effective manager (EM)* and the "partnerships" they forge with their employees. Effective managers foster diversity and practice inclusion well in order to motivate and develop the "people" who are driving their business and organization.

What happens when (effective) managers develop, value, empower and respect employees? *Employees feel valued and respected, increase their productivity and engagement levels!*

Effective managers challenge their employees with continuous improvement thinking and create development opportunities to help them gain the knowledge and expertise they need to serve the customers, create a positive workplace and improve business results.

Feeling valued, respected, developed, empowered and treated fairly, results in "people" becoming *engaged employees (E2)*. They come to work each day, usually earlier than expected, display a positive attitude toward their work, co-workers, manager and the organization. They communicate openly, offer constructive suggestions, and get things done – right and on time!

What happens when employees are productive and engaged? *They provide finer customer service and achieve better results for themselves, their team and their organization!*

Engaged employees, then, engage their customers by building solid, deep professional relationships with them. *Engaged customers (EC),* in turn, feel valued, respected, treated fairly and bring in more business.

Customer expectations – both the *internal* (employees) and *external* customer (paying) – are the same – they, too, expect those who they interact with to treat them fairly, with respect, to be friendly, and to make them feel valued. You will earn their respect, their return and receive more referral business. They can become your best ambassadors!

A few years ago, Harvard Business School did some research about the link between fair treatment and profitability. Here's what their research found:
- When HR indicators (like coming to work, absenteeism, # of CHRO complaints, etc.) were high – customer satisfaction was low.
- When HR indicators were low – customer satisfaction was high.

What's the bottom-line? Creating a positive workplace is critical to an organization's success. Effective managers are those people who are in the right management position that allows them to use their talents, skills and experience to the highest good in building positive workplace environments that develop and engage their most important asset – the people!

How does your workplace stack-up? If you are a "people manager," what are your employees saying about you?

A Positive Workplace
Means Business!
It Just Makes Cent$! TM

Chapter Eight

Networking: Turning Small Talk into Positive Business-Talk

Do you have a networking strategy? Does your strategy involve more than just making contacts? If you answered "No" to one or both of these questions, it's time for a "Networking Check-Up."

Just as location, location, location is the key element in real estate transactions, networking, networking, networking is the key element in any business development plan. Whether your business is large or small, a start-up or one with a long-history, for-profit or not-for-profit, networking is the key to business development!

Sounds simple, right? Why then do so many people struggle with networking events? Why do people find it difficult to introduce themselves to strangers and make small talk at social events? Successful networking involves more than just making contacts. Making contacts is more than just attending networking events and collecting business cards. It's all about the people-to-people ("P2P") connections!

Turning small talk into *positive business-talk* depends on developing and following a strategic networking plan to fit your career and personal goals. There is no one-size-fits-all process. Your strategic networking plan begins with a *positive* attitude and an honest look or "check-up" (self-assessment) of your networking skills. It will be as unique as you are.

Your personal networking plan will be designed to maximize your personal and professional strengths – and your own networking style! According to author and networking guru, Nancy Flynn, some key areas to think about include:

- ➤ **Goals** – Your reasons for improving or enhancing your networking skills
- ➤ **Contacts** – Your access to the "right people" at the right time
- ➤ **Personal style** – Your comfort level and listening skills and the impression you make
- ➤ **Tools and techniques** – Your experience and comfort level with publicity, public speaking, e-mail, and other networking tools
- ➤ **Resources** – Your ability to devote time, energy, and financial resources to networking and career development
- ➤ **Etiquette and netiquette** – Your know-how and savvy can make or break the deal
- ➤ **Challenges** – Your personal and professional development areas
- ➤ **Commitment** – Your desire to succeed and willingness to follow through

Most likely you already have some networking skills and will discover other areas that need to be explored or fine-tuned. It's important to clarify your networking needs and goals and be realistic as you look at your strengths and development areas. Breaking your "check-up" into the following key target areas will help you easily determine what needs to be explored, developed or fine-tuned:

1. Identifying Focus & Setting Goals (Include appropriate networking events and activities in your business/marketing plan)

2. Relationship-Building Skills (Need a professional skills coach?)
3. People Skills (Attend a local workshop)
4. Networking Tools & Techniques (Join a networking group to learn from others)
5. Networking Challenges (Be honest with yourself – there are ways to make it work)

Once you have completed your "check-up" and have determined your personal plan, you are on your way to becoming a successful networker! It's about taking the time to invest in yourself and your business. You will learn to start and grow relationships with people who can open doors, make introductions, advance your career and help build your business by establishing long-term, reciprocal relationships with the "right" people.

Who are the "right" people? They are not necessarily the wealthiest, most powerful, or most senior executives in town. Surely, these people are good to have as a part of your networking strategy. Just remember to include all types of people who understand how the networking game is played and are willing to help you get into the action.

If you look at networking as a "two-way street"– a giving and receiving tool - your success as a receiver will be as great as your *generosity as a giver*. Like a smile, give it away, and it will come back to you in ways that you'd never imagine.
Here are a few tips that work for me:
- Be generous with information
- Share your contacts
- Help people help other people
- Do favors
- Ask for help

- And most importantly, thank those who have helped you!

When you do, you will find people will be ready and willing to open doors, offer tips, make the introductions and connections for you in return.

How Do You Do?

Many of us work with large numbers of people, not just our customers but also suppliers, vendors, and other partners in the supply chain. Every industry and country has its own conventions to help people meet others and establish good working relationships. Here are some tips for introducing and addressing people when you meet them for the first time.

1. In the United States, once you have been introduced to a person, you can use first names for almost everyone in your own company no matter how many layers of management are between you.

2. First names are considered too familiar even between colleagues in Europe, unless you are invited to use them. Instead, use the person's courtesy title (such as *Monsieur* or *Madame*) and last name.

3. Be aware that introductions are more formal and more important in Europe and Asia than in the United States.

4. Always introduce the less senior person to the more senior person first. If Ms. Pontini is the CEO, for example, you would introduce the new receptionist by saying, "Ms. Pontini, I'd like you

to meet Mr. Hamilton. Mr. Hamilton, this is Ms. Pontini."

5.   Whether in the United States or abroad, always stand to introduce or be introduced to anyone, and *smile*. It shows you are interested in and respect them.

6.   If it is appropriate to shake hands, do so firmly. Find out what gestures are considered appropriate overseas. Does a bow need to accompany a handshake? Does a handshake conclude with an embrace?

7.   Begin meetings by making sure appropriate introductions are made so everyone knows each other.

8.   Find out the correct business titles of those you will be meeting or introducing, and if necessary, practice the proper pronunciation of their names. Could be embarrassing for you and offensive for the other person(s).

9.   Understand the appropriate and acceptable physical distances between people in other cultures. Some stand closer together when conversing than is common in the United States and others a little farther apart.

10.   Business cards are more important abroad than in the United States. Accept them graciously and treat them with care. It's a nice touch to print your own cards in English on one side and on the other side in the language of the country you are visiting; present the card foreign-language side up.

How to Remember Names

It happens to all of us! You're out of your element and bump into someone on the street, in the library, in a dorm lounge, or in a restaurant – and you draw a complete blank. You know this person, and yet you can't remember his or her name! So, if you're like me, I greet them with a big smile and say, "Hi there!" In business, it is especially important to remember people's names – not just your boss and co-workers, but customers, suppliers, and colleagues in other divisions. Here are a few tips to help you:

1. When you first meet someone, repeat his or her name several times, which will help engrave the name and face together in your memory. You don't have to be obvious about it. You can say, "It's a pleasure to meet you, Gabrielle," and "I hope to see you again, Paula."

2. If appropriate, ask the person one or two questions that will help you to lock the details in your memory. Questions such as, "Do you live in town?" or even, "Where did you go to college?" help establish a more complete picture of the person.

3. Try associating the person with other people – for example was he or she part of a group when you were introduced? Were you introduced by a mutual friends or colleague? Also try to associate the location or circumstances of your introduction – at a restaurant, in a conference room, at an association meeting.

4. Without being obvious, pick a feature about the person that stands out – jet-black hair, a bright red tie, an unusual purse. Later you can mentally attach the feature to the name. This will help you create a mental picture of the person.

5. If you scroll through your mental picture, association with others, and individual details and you still can't come up with the person's name, simply reintroduce yourself. It works for me! Saying, "Hello, I'm Mary Jane Paris," usually prompts the person to respond with a similar reintroduction. If not, and you've only met the person briefly once before, it's ok to go ahead and ask for his or her name again. Be sure to listen carefully and apply some of the memory cures listed, so next time that name won't be stuck on the tip of your tongue.

   Positive business-talk reinforces the fact that people do business with those they know, like and trust. Networking is *positively* the best way to reach out and hold on to people who can make things happen – in a fraction of the time it would take you to accomplish the same goals on your own. As noted by (SHRM) the Society for Human Resource Management, 95% of human resource professionals and job seekers claim networking is the most effective tool to locate job candidates or secure a job.

   Who's in your networking circle? Cast a wide net to include family, friends, co-workers, alumni groups, teachers, students, chamber members, civic and professional organizations, just a few of the many possibilities. Becoming a successful networker does not require being the most extroverted person in town – people skills can be learned. It does require focusing clearly on your career and business goals and implementing a networking strategy to take you there. By pursuing only the networking activities, business relationships, and professional skills that will move you closer to personal, career and business success, you will make a *Positive Impact* on the lives of others and the communities you serve.

Invest in yourself with a networking check-up! Go out of your comfort zone! Connect with people as much as you can! It's all about "P2P" once again. As the phone company used to say, reach out and talk to someone! Turn small talk into *positive business-talk!*

A Positive Workplace
Means Business!
It Just Makes Cent$! TM

Chapter Nine

Face-to-Face Communication
Old Fashioned? Not!

It's unbelievable how dependent we've become as a society on electronic communication devices! E-mail, text messaging, PDA's, cell phones, video conferencing, blackberries, blueberries, rasberries, and more have taken the place of good old fashioned, face-to-face communication leading to many interpersonal difficulties and miscommunications in today's workplace.

You may be thinking…Why improve my interpersonal skills when most businesses do 99% of communication by telephone, teleconferencing, videoconferencing, e-mail, and on rare occasions, snail mail. A popular way of thinking today…but, is it really the correct way? "Face-to-face communication remains the most powerful human interaction," says Kathleen Begley, Ed.D., author of *Face-to-Face Communication, Making Human Connections in a Technology-Driven World.* "As wonderful as electronic devices are, they can never fully replace the intimacy and immediacy of people conversing in the same room and it has worked for millions of years."

In business, we talk about "B2B" (business to business) and "B2C" (business to consumer) methods. In the workshops and community college classes that I teach, I try to buck the trend (in a positive way!) to stress the importance of face-to-face communication. You'll hear me talk a lot about the "P2P" (people-to-people) connections and how important it is to get beyond technology and talk face-to-face with friends, family, colleagues, customers, vendors, and the like. You may think that's a bit old-fashioned, but in my opinion, there is no substitution for the human, up-close and personal contact. Don't get me wrong, there is a place for the terrific technology tools we have today and I use it regularly, but it's not always my first or best choice.

Several decades ago, John Naisbitt, in his mega 1960's best-seller, *Megatrends: Ten New Directions Transforming Our Lives*, brought a new concept to the forefront called "high tech, high touch." His idea was that "as human beings became capable of anonymous electronic communication, they would concurrently need more close-up personal interaction." Seems to me that he was right on target!

We live in a society when flocking to the local coffee shop or diner for coffee chats with business associates or friends is a testimony to our need for human togetherness, especially when most coffee lovers can make a latte or cappuccino right in their homes. Think about the fortunes coffee establishments are making on our need for face-to-face communication! The people-to-people (P2P") connections…

We hear of the many children (and adults) who spend countless hours alone playing video games. However, The Game Manufacturing Association reported in 2003 that family board game sales (like Monopoly and Scrabble) are booming and growing at 20% per year. Cranium has recently come out with a whole new line of board games for our "little people" (ages 3+). The people-to-people connections start at an early age – if you haven't heard it, ask me to tell you my "Papa Zitto" story!

Even when disaster strikes and the news media brings these events into our homes and workplaces via TV, radio and the Internet, we seek out opportunities to share grief. I personally waited in line for almost three hours with hundreds of others to visit Ground Zero in New York when it opened to the public in December 2001. Many people also left tokens nearby to honor the victims of that tragedy. The people-to-people ("P2P") connections...

We lead hectic, multi-tasking lives both at home and in the workplace these days and we find the need for balance even more critical than in days gone by. We understand that technology can be impersonal, but it's quick! We know we need to make time for more people-to-people connections but, the reality of the hectic pace doesn't leave us much time for this more intimate form of communication. You may be thinking, isn't it much faster to make a quick phone call, send a brief e-mail, or hook up via video-conferencing to have a meeting of the minds? Yes and no. It's a communications paradox...faster is not always better.

So the better question may be, how can we make the best of both worlds - technology and face-to-face, people-to-people connections?

Just as fashions are redesigned and come back with a variation on a style from days-gone- by, I believe it is time for redesigning and revitalizing face-to-face ("P2P") communication skills.

We need to get the balance right! Face-to-face, ("F2F"), people-to-people ("P2P") communication skills remain one of the primary success factors in business, even in this age of technology. There are many situations – often those involving conflict, hurt feelings, high priority, or a large sum of money – that demand business people take the time and trouble to get in the same room to share information. Video-conferencing has become a good simulation and cost-effective method when individuals are in remote locations, but there is still no substitute for good, old-fashioned, face-to-face communication.

Don't take my word for it…Let's take a look at what some of the experts are saying.

Tom Peters, internationally known business guru, says without reservation that you should constantly attend to your face-to-face communication. Not to do so, will lead to career disaster. "We believe in high tech, high touch," Peters writes. "No question, technology is the Great Enabler. But, paradoxically, now the human bit is more, not less, important than ever before."

Sheila Hodge, author of *Global Smarts: The Art of Communicating and Deal Making Anywhere in the World,* says "The modern office is full of gadgets – computers and the Internet, uplinks and downlinks, videoconferencing, and online databases. Many people think they should let the fancy technology handle the messy task of interfacing with people."

Jo-Ellan Dimitrius, in her book *Reading People,* talks about how young, technically oriented employees tend to communicate mostly in computer chat rooms. "If you want to become a better communicator, you must make a conscious effort to engage other people (in person)," she writes. "Even the most entrenched Internet junkie can learn the true meaning of 'chat' if the desire is there, but you have to get off the couch and make it happen."

Gary McClain and Deborah Romaine in their book, *The Everything Managing People Book*, put it this way…"Consistent, daily face-to-face communication promotes more than just good feelings; it also promotes effective and collaborative teamwork."

"One of the most critical areas of communication to get right in business is the one-on-one situations – especially offering advice, constructive feedback, and annual performance appraisals," says Chris Roebuck in *Effective Communication.*

One of my favorite quotes stated very simply by Margaret Wheatley, *Turning to One Another: Simple Conversations to Restore Hope for the Future,* says "I can believe we can change the world if we start talking to one another again."

Sounds like we're on to something here…So, what can you do? Start out by taking an honest look at your communication methods and your attitude about technology vs. face-to-face interaction. Are you e-mailing more and meeting less for financial reasons? Are you avoiding human contact mostly because of a lack of interpersonal skills? If the latter is true, you need to take action before it's too late.

The next time you are tempted to send an e-mail, text message or make a phone call for other than routine purposes, stop! Get back to basics. Go out of your comfort zone and, instead, send the e-mail, text message or make the call to set up a face-to-face, in person meeting with the person behind the technology! Why? Because it works!

Remember to make the people-to-people
("P2P") connections…
You and your business will be glad you did!

A Positive Workplace
Means Business!
It Just Makes Cent$! ᴛᴍ

Chapter Ten

Positive Energy
Stress Management on the Job

When we talk about the Positive Workplace, we must include the affects of stress on ourselves and on our employees, if we are people managers that contribute to job burnout.

Workplace stress continues to grow. But, *remember it is manageable, workable, and reversible.*

This is the time of the year when many people, especially those in the accounting profession, begin to feel their shoulders droop, their patience running thin, their hearts racing more often and just feel overwhelmed & stressed much of the time! Right?

Even if you are not in the accounting profession, this may still describe how you feel. Some of us get stressed at just the thought of trying to fit one more thing into our already busy balancing act!

Before we talk about some interesting information and tips about managing stress and related job burnout, try this quick de-stressor "Office Yoga" exercise to get you focused.

1. Raise your arms straight up above your head.

2. Flap your hands really fast.

3. Breathe in and out quickly.

(Do this for as long as you can manage -- or until your coworkers notice.)

Feel a little more relaxed? Just the laughter will help you to perk-up!

Some of you might be thinking, "A Positive Workplace" – Are you kidding, MJ? You don't know what it's like! My response to you is, "Oh, yes I do!" I have spent many a stressful day building a career, raising two sons as a single parent, providing elderly out-of-state parents with care and support, living thru down-sizing, right–sizing, wrong-sizing, finishing my education in the evening and, for the past few years, building my business. I used to be six-feet tall!

Working at a desk can be more stressful to your body than you may think. Spending long periods of time in a desk chair can cause your circulation to slow down, meaning your muscles aren't getting enough oxygen, and that often results in muscle tension. And if you have the added stress of a type-A-personality boss, you could be on your way to a major ibuprofen moment.

This stress can carry over into your personal life as well, resulting in increased anxiety and even sleepless nights. Most everyone knows some of the standard stress management techniques: limiting caffeine, exercise, soothing music, warm baths, 15 minute naps, visual aids, etc. Some of these we can use at work, others we need to practice at a spa, gym or at home.

There is, however, another aspect of stress management that's important to talk about – *self-talk!* Dr. Dru Scott (Ph.D.), noted researcher and author of "Stress That Motivates," says, "Most people have never been told about the connection between stress, motivation and self-talk."

"The Big Connection," he says, is that our self-talk contributes to most of our stress (and job burnout) – something maybe you haven't thought about before today. What we say to ourselves about a situation will either stress or motivate us!

Make sense? How many of you are aware of your own self-talk each day? How much of it is positive? Negative?

Remember…We all have choices and control over what we think and what we do!

Job burnout, if not recognized and dealt with, can progress until a person dreads going to work. Even worse, burnout tends to spread to all aspects of a person's life. Rarely is a person burned out at work, yet energized and enthusiastic at home.

Did you know?

- More than 50% of adult Americans suffer adverse health effects due to stress.
- Medical researchers estimate that up to 90% of illness and disease is stress-related.
- Stress is linked to the six leading causes of death: heart disease, cancer, lung ailments, accidents, cirrhosis of the liver, and suicide.
- Stress has a huge effect on bottom-line results in the workplace in terms of employees' health and vitality, capacity for critical thinking, innovative competencies, and competitiveness.

In the U.S., experts at the Centers for Disease Control and the National Institute for Occupational Safety and Health are dedicated to studying stress and have found the following to be true:

Did you know?

- More than 3 out of 5 doctors' office visits are for stress related problems
- The Occupational Safety and Health Administration (OSHA) has declared stress a hazard of the workplace
- Health care costs account for about 12% of the gross domestic product, and that number is rising.
- Job burnout experienced by 25% to 40% of U.S. workers is blamed on stress.
- More than ever before, employee stress is being recognized as a major drain on corporate productivity and competitiveness.
- Depression, only one type of stress reaction, is predicted to be the leading occupational disease of the 21st century, responsible for more days lost than any other single factor.
- $300 billion, or $7,500 per employee, is spent annually in the U.S. on stress-related compensation claims, reduced productivity, absenteeism, health insurance costs, direct medical expenses (nearly 50% higher for workers who report stress), and employee turnover.

Did you know high-stress employees show:

- More than double the rate of heart and cardiovascular problems (stressful workplace conditions are said to be the equivalent of smoking, being overweight, being unfit, and eating poorly)
- Significantly higher rates of anxiety, depression and demoralization
- Significantly higher rates of alcohol and prescription/over-the-counter drug abuse

- Significantly higher levels of susceptibility to a wide range of infectious diseases
- Higher incidences of back pain (up to 3 times higher)
- And higher incidences of repetitive strain injuries (up to 2.5 times higher)

If you or someone you know answers "yes" to having one or more of these warning signals, please seek help!

- Feelings of frustration
- Emotional outbursts
- "Why bother?" attitude
- Sense of alienation
- Substandard performance
- Increased use of alcohol and drugs

So, what's the #1 way to manage stress and job burnout?

Awareness: Tuning in to our "chatter" and "thoughts." Be aware of the messages you are sending yourself when you are under stress. Are they alarming or reassuring? You can decrease your stress by learning to talk to yourself in a reassuring way. Be aware of your "stress-building" beliefs about perfectionism, control, people-pleasing and competence. Practice *Positive Self-Talk!* This is what "stress-busting" is about--getting your thoughts back on a reassuring track.

Challenge your beliefs! Experiment! Try acting in a way that is opposite to your usual behavior. Then, evaluate the results.

Did your "dimmer switch" get turned up a notch or two? Become more aware about recognizing and cutting stress, add energy and get the right things done – by changing the way you talk to yourselves!

Remember…The workplace environment drives employees. Employees drive your business. This thing called "stress" has a great affect on our workplace environment, results and the bottom-line!

Be good to yourself and think good thoughts!

A Positive Workplace
Means Business!
It Just Makes Cent$! TM

Chapter Eleven

Making Humor Work

You probably get it by now…the "Positive Workplace" and the importance of giving time and energy into the people who are really driving our businesses – the employees – is what I stand for!

I firmly believe that the road to results is through our employees. The attitude we bring to the workplace each day sets the tone for a positive, productive work environment or a negative, toxic one. The manager-employee relationship and their ultimate connection with the internal and external customers, vendors, suppliers – *the people-to-people ("P2P") connections* - will either make or break your organization.

Let me give you some recent statistics about the people in our U.S. workplaces according to The Society for Human Relationship Management's (SHRM) August 2007 HR Magazine and a recent (February 2007) Conference Board survey, employee satisfaction has reached all time lows.

- Less than half of Americans say they are satisfied with their jobs, down from 61% 20 years ago.
- Workers under 25 were the most dissatisfied; while workers ages 45 – 54 expressed the second lowest level (45%).

According to a poll taken by CCH HR Management in October 2006, absenteeism is up in

US workplaces and that there was a direct association with absenteeism and employee morale.

- Nearly twice as many companies with "Poor/Fair" morale reported an increase in unscheduled absences over the past two years compared to companies with "Good/Very Good" morale (33% vs. 17%)
- Moreover, 46% of companies with low morale reported that unscheduled absenteeism is a serious problem for them.

Chances are, when you think about your workplace…you may also be experiencing some or all of these issues.

Have you thought about what the difference is between employee satisfaction and employee morale?

Employee satisfaction is about how employees feel about their particular duties; employee morale refers to how they feel about the company they are working for.

When we talk about the people who are driving our businesses and creating a more positive workplace, we need to include how we uplift these employees. Raising and maintaining employee morale takes sincere communications and respect, and yes, some appropriate humor. Often companies where morale is low try quick fixes like giving raises or new benefits or holding employee events, but that won't work over the long run!

Boosting employee morale starts with knowing where morale stands. What is the best way to find out where morale stands? Many organizations do an employee survey. Then what? The well-run, positive workplaces get that data into the hands of managers and give those managers the responsibility to feed it back to their employees and create effective action plans.

What's next? They measure behavior! Track the kinds of actions people are taking, the schedule for meeting their goals, and the percentage of managers who are accomplishing their action items. These are statistics that you can report to your executives and that your executives can exert some control over – because they can control leaders, but not attitudes.

Managers need help with understanding how career and lifestyle events impact employees and that there's a liability in not getting close with your employees.

Good morale depends on effective top management, says John Gerhard, executive director of Boston-based law firm, Nixon Peabody, LLP. The firm was one of Fortune magazine's 100 Best Companies to Work for in 2007 and was noted for its low turnover. "Often poor morale is a reflection of the inattention of top management to the people in the organization," he says.

On to the subject of humor…There is much to learn about your sense of humor and how it can work for you.

When a comedian uses humor, we're always asking "Is it funny?" When you use humor in the business world, the question is different. You are asking, "Does it work?"

Do you think *you* use appropriate humor on the job or in your volunteer work, at home, etc? There is great value when humor is used properly, especially in the business world. It can increase your personal and professional effectiveness, and also the effectiveness of others. Humor can disarm anger and defuse resistance to change while still promoting problem solving. Most importantly, humor can help you develop more self-confidence and manage stress in an ever-changing world.

Humor can help your organization, to run smoother, cut medical costs, increase sales and production levels, and even polish the company or organization's public image.

A benefit on any job is laughter. It should never be a crime to have fun on the job; it may very well be a crime not to. And best of all, it doesn't cost a penny!

Most of us have become far too serious! We have people who are better trained than ever, but they don't seem to have nearly as much fun as they once did.

U.S. workers, for example, consume over 15 tons of aspirin a day! With all the down-sizing, right-sizing, mergers, acquisitions, etc., survivor syndrome has set in across all sectors. Baby boomers have begun exiting organizations, a trend that will only continue over the next 10 years, leaving gaps in intellectual property, skills and a work ethic that is hard to beat.

As if our own personal and professional lives were not stressful enough, we are besieged with a steady diet of depressing local, national and world news! Do you watch the evening news? How do you feel after? The media guarantees to bring any world or national crisis to your doorstop the same day. If there are no catastrophes, do not despair. There is usually a supply of footage from old tragedies to celebrate anniversaries of pain.

It's no better on the job! Reorganizations, corporate buyouts, and global competition are causing workers to work harder, change, or fall behind. It's no wonder stress related illnesses are filling our doctor's offices.

As a result, many of us have lost touch with the importance of fun in the workplace. We move through life with flat expressions on our faces. Take a minute and think about the people on the job that look like they are in pain most of the day! Before you laugh too hard, think if others might put you on their list!

It is dangerous to confuse professionalism with seriousness. You can take your job and your world seriously, and still take yourself lightly! Human beings are by nature spontaneous and playful creatures. Yet the older we become, the less appropriate it seems for us to allow it to be expressed.

The good news is that humor – laughter- is proven to reduce stress! So why aren't we doing more of it?

Think about the best place you have worked for over the years and what made it the best? Chances are having fun at work was one of the factors!

Don't get me wrong! Making your work environment a "comedy store" is not making humor work! It is an abuse of an organization's time when important work is not being done. Work hard. Laugh hard. Misplaced humor can be counterproductive and distracting. But life on the job or at home without laughter is also not the answer.

As the old saying goes, laughter may be the best medicine!

 - Laughter is a non-fattening, contagious, pleasant tranquilizer without side affects
 - Laughter can interrupt the panic cycle of an illness and actually promote healing
 - Well placed humor can break the urgency cycle and create a different, less stressful perception
 - Humor will help you to build and maintain positive human relationships

Remember...He who laughs, lasts! Here's hoping that you last too, and that you laugh a little along the way for fun and profit!

The important thing to remember is that we all have a job to do. But we can have fun along the way...and make it a more positive workplace for ourselves and our employees!

A Positive Workplace Means Business! It Just Makes Cent$! TM

Chapter Twelve

Etiquette in the Workplace

Etiquette is more important than ever in today's workplace! Given the close proximity of people in the workplace, technology tools and their affect on our time, the global business culture, and the on-going social and networking interactions, we live in a hectic, fast-paced business world! We can easily forget about the importance of etiquette appropriate communication in developing and maintaining the people-to-people ("P2P") connections.

It doesn't matter whether we are self-employed, or work for a small business, not-for-profit, educational institution or large corporation, we all need to remember the basics and keep it simple to survive and thrive in the 21st century.

Research has proven what we already know - that negative, toxic environments driven by a lack of etiquette and inappropriate communication from leaders, disengage and de-motivate employees, while positive, supportive environments built upon respect, engage and motivate our most valuable asset – the people. Higher engagement and productivity leads to higher quality of service and improved results.

We also know that no workplace will ever be perfect, as we, the people working there, are not perfect! We can, however, do our personal best each day to make it as positive as possible.

I'd like to share some of my research and findings to help you to remember…*A Positive Workplace Means…*

Being Considerate of Co-Workers

Are you a "cube dweller?" If you find yourself occupying a cubicle, here are some ways to ensure that you are as considerate of others as you would wish them to be of you.

1. Respect the privacy of others. Imagine that cubicles have full walls and doors; avoid glancing in when you walk by and always knock before entering. If the person you need to see is busy, don't wait in the doorway; come back later.

2. When you are in someone else's office or cube, keep your eyes off the computer screen or top of the desk. If the other person's phone rings, excuse yourself and come back later.

3. If listening to music is permitted while working, wear head phones to avoid distracting others.

4. Set the volume low on your computer, and use a screen saver option without sound affects.

5. Answer your phone promptly (usually three rings) and keep your voice down. Set the ring tone and speakerphone volume on low. If you must make a personal call, remember that you can probably be heard.

6. Be aware that some people are sensitive to strong or excessive perfumes, colognes, and sprays, and apply them sparingly and before you leave home.

7. Keep personal touches to your space in line with company standards and take care not to offend or distract co-workers, clients, or other visitors with inappropriate posters, cartoons, or trinkets.

8. If an impromptu meeting or gathering begins outside someone's workspace, move to a conference room or common area to avoid disturbing others.

9. If you need to borrow something from another person's office, ask permission first, and always return or replace the item.

10. Avoid habits that distract others, such as popping gum, humming, tapping things on the desk, taking shoes off, eating food with strong odors, and leaving trash and leftovers out.

Handling Interruptions

Managers at all levels of an organization are interrupted every few minutes every day to deal with important – and sometimes not-so-important – issues. Interruptions are part of a manager's day, and they simply can't be avoided. So here are some suggestions for dealing with them tactfully.

1. If someone stops by just to chat, say something friendly but unmistakable, such as, "I don't have time to talk right now. Can we catch up later?"

2. Do you have some persistent visitors? Discourage them by getting up and moving away from your desk, by picking up some work or positioning yourself in front of your computer, or even by excusing yourself to go to the restroom.

3. Remove extra chairs from your office or cubicle to make it a less inviting place for others to kill time.

4. If you really need a block of time without interruptions, ask your staff and co-workers to respect that time, forward your phone calls, turn off your cell phone, and, if you have a door, close it.

5. Some interruptions are unintentional, such as the noise of others in the hallway. If they interfere with a meeting or phone call, consider requesting the use of a conference room for a set period of time. Once there, turn off your cell phone and close the door.

6. When an interruption to a meeting or interview is expected and can't be avoided, explain in advance to those attending and arrange to make the break as short as possible.

7. If the only way you can handle phone interruptions to a meeting is by answering the phone, answer promptly, thank the person for calling, get a call-back number, and say, "I'm meeting with someone now, but I'll get back to you right after the meeting," and be sure to do so.

8. Be considerate and avoid letting interruptions make the person standing or sitting in front of you feel less important.

9. Keep your cell phone or pager in "vibrate" mode and wear it. Noisy vibrations against a table or desktop defeat the purpose of silencing the device.

10. Avoid creating interruption issues for others by asking yourself before phoning them whether they really need to hear from you right now. If not, call later.

Working Effectively with Service Providers

Tips on Business Tipping

When we eat out, take a cab, or stay in a hotel, we're faced with some common dilemmas. Whom – and how much – should you tip? If you find tipping a mystery, here are a few guidelines to help you solve the puzzle.

- At a restaurant, it is customary to tip your waiter between 15 – 20 percent of the bill. You may calculate the tip before tax or alcohol, but many people simply base the tip on the total bill. Naturally, if the service is outstanding, you'll want to tip at the upper end of the scale.
- If you check coat(s) at a restaurant or event, tip the person $1 per coat.
- Tip the bellhop $1 to $2 per bag for carrying your luggage.
- Give a valet or parking attendant $1 to $2 for parking or retrieving your car.
- Add a 10 to 15 percent tip to the fare for a taxi ride, or $1 to $2 for a free shuttle.
- If the hotel concierge provides you with special service such as arranging a meeting space or making dinner or theater reservations, tip that person around $5.
- If he/she has provided an extraordinary service, a tip of $20 is not out of line.

Of course, before you tip, make sure that a service charge has not already been included. Some upscale restaurants and hotels have begun automatically including fees ranging up to 20 percent.

While these guidelines should be helpful, before you make any calculations, remember that service personnel usually try their best to make your experience a good one. "When in doubt, I always operate under the premise that you tip for a service performed with excellence, and you tip more generously for something that exceeds your expectations," advises Amy Ziff of Travelocity Business. "And remember the saying, 'what goes around comes around,' and that in business a little good tipping karma can never hurt."

Dining for Dollars

Entrepreneurs need money to fund their businesses. Many start with their own savings, but they quickly reach a point at which outside financing is necessary to survive and grow. So being successful means becoming skilled in attracting potential investors. Often the initial courtship occurs over a business meal, which can be a good way to get to know each other in a relaxed setting. But the dinner requires some savvy etiquette. To unravel the mystery of dining for dollars, follow these hints from the experts.

- Before setting up a dinner meeting, think through the mission of the meal. Is it simply to introduce yourself and your business? Are you ready to discuss specific business details? Write down your objectives.

- If possible, choose a restaurant you already know, where you trust the food and the staff. You'll want someplace that is relatively quiet so that you can talk. If you are paying a visit to potential investors outside your own town, research the restaurants ahead of time. You can ask your guests where they would like to eat – but make it clear that you will be the host.

- Arrive at the restaurant ten to fifteen minutes before the reservation time. Let the restaurant host know you are there. Wait in the lobby or near the door for your guests. If the staff prefers to seat you at the table, do not order drinks or food until your guests arrive.

- Greet your guests upon arrival with a smile and a firm handshake. Keep business papers off the table, and turn off your cell phone. Enjoy the dinner and follow proper dining etiquette. Limit your alcohol intake, and don't smoke.

- Don't skip dessert and coffee. Key business discussions often take place during this part of the meal. It is usually acceptable to refer to any documents you my need for discussion at this point.

- When the check arrives, payment is your responsibility. Do so quickly and quietly. Alternatively, if you arrive early enough, you can give the wait staff your credit card so that it is clear you will be paying the bill.

- Escort your guests to the door, shake hands, and thank them for taking the time to join you. Later, you may want to jot down some meeting notes. Send a written note to your guests within a day or two, thanking them again for their time and consideration.

Telephone and Technology Tools

Minding Your Telephone Manners

It's all too easy to forget the importance of the impression we make over the telephone. But that link is as critical for businesses as face-to-face communication.

To ensure that your telephone conversations at work send the right message about you and your firm, check out the following guidelines.

1. Answer your own phone whenever possible, and answer promptly – by the third ring.

2. Say, "Hello, this is (your name) speaking," or a variation that is preferred in your workplace or department.

3. If the caller has the wrong number, be courteous when acknowledging the error and hanging up. If you think you can redirect the call for the person, offer to do so first. Likewise, if you dial a wrong number, apologize briefly and hang up.

4. Reduce background noise when using the phone to avoid distractions and to convey the message that the caller is your first priority.

5. Return all calls within 24 hours. The only exception is urgent calls, which you should return immediately.

6. Speak slowly, clearly, and in a pleasant tone. Smile when you speak – it conveys a positive attitude even if the other person can't see you.

7. If you are taking a call for someone else, give as little detail as possible about where the person is and offer to either take a message or transfer the caller to a voice-mail system. If you take a message, get complete information, including the time of the call; write clearly; and make sure the message is delivered promptly.

8. When you make a call, dial carefully, identify yourself, and ask for the party to whom you wish to speak.

9. Prepare what you need to say ahead of time and get to the point. Be considerate of others' time.

10. Remember that you may be working with people who live in different time zones from yours. Make sure you call during their regular working hours, not yours.

Tips for Using E-Mail
You are probably aware of the general guidelines about using e-mail responsibly, such as following the rules of grammar and spelling, not typing in all caps, and not sending anyone information you wouldn't

mind seeing in the daily newspaper. Here are a few tips that should help you construct effective and appropriate online business correspondence.

1. Choose a professional-looking format; avoid color, fancy type fonts, and emoticons (smiley faces).

2. Keep your message short and to the point.

3. Always include a specific subject line so that your correspondents know what to expect.

4. If you are replying to an e-mail, respond as promptly as you would to a phone call on the same subject.

5. Write and reply to all the people who need the information you are sending, but only to those people.

6. If you are writing to a large group of people who don't know one another, use the BCC (blind carbon copy) function to ensure that each person's e-mail address remains private from the others.

7. Let recipients know ahead of time if you are sending a very large attachment, because download times can vary. You might want to break large attachments into several smaller ones to make downloading easier.

8. If a disagreement or argument develops during e-mail communications, stop, breath, calm down, and continue the discussion in person or on the phone.

9. Before you send any e-mail, proofread your message and double-check the "To:" line. Make sure you have attached any needed documents and that you've typed your name at the bottom of the message.

10. Remember that e-mails are considered public documents. Avoid writing anything you wouldn't say in person.

When – and How – to Use Your Computer and Electronic Devices at Work

These days, having access to a computer or other electronic device is standard operating procedure.

Whether you're in sales, marketing, finance, or human resources, a computer will, no doubt, be nearby – if not actually on your desk then in your pocket or purse in the form of a Blackberry, blueberry or raspberry! You already know what your computer/electronic device is for: *work!*

Despite this fact, one recent survey revealed that 93 percent of workers who had a computer or other electronic device at work also used it for personal purposes – e-mailing, texting or accessing the Web. The most popular sites accessed were news, personal e-mail, online banks, travel companies, and shopping. Gaming has also soared in popularity. Microsoft's game site, www.Zone.com, reports its busiest time of day is mid-afternoon Eastern time – when most people are at work.

While this practice may seem harmless, businesses that allow employees to surf the Internet freely may face serious consequences. An employer may be held legally responsible for employees' misuse of e-mail – such as bullying, threatening, or making sexual explicit comments. A firm is also vulnerable to disclosure of its private information, as well as viruses spread via e-mail. Then there's the lost productivity of employees who are gaming and shopping during work time. So before you log on at work, consider the following:

- Make sure you know your company's policy about computer and Internet use. One firm might allow casual e-mailing or shopping during lunch hours; another might not. If you violate the policy, you could find yourself unemployed. If your firm doesn't have a formal policy, ask your supervisor for guidelines before you log on. Then use common sense.

- If you may use your computer for some personal messages, be aware that most firms can monitor employee e-mail. "Employees should avoid pretty much anything they wouldn't want to print out and hang up on their cubicle walls," warns one technology consultant.

- Be honest about whether you really need to use the Internet during the workday. If you need to make a quick bank deposit online or check the time of your next flight, fine. But if you're surfing the Web for a great pair of shoes to wear next weekend, save it for after work.

Every firm is different, but "the solution lies in balancing employees' needs for personal use of the

Web at work without draining overall productivity," advises Geoff Haggart of Internet firm Websense.

The Personal Touch

Thank-You Notes Do Count

When someone gives you a gift – whether it is an item wrapped and tied with a bow, a home-cooked meal, or even some career advice on the phone – it is appropriate to acknowledge the person's time and effort with a thank-you note. After a job interview, it is customary to write a thank-you note as well. As a former corporate recruiter, the well-written thank-you may not have landed the job for some, but it certainly set candidates apart from one another!

If you're like most people, you're hit with a huge case of writer's block the minute you sit down with a blank thank-you note. Maybe you've delayed your note writing until you forgot what you were thanking the person for, or until so much time had passed that you were embarrassed to write at all. But "thank you" may be the two most important words you'll ever say to someone, and you can write a brief note in just a few minutes. You'll be glad you did, and so will the recipient.

Here are a few tips to help:

1. Handwrite your note, even if it is career related. A handwritten note takes a bit more time and effort, so it conveys both warmth and sincerity. Use simple notepaper and blue or black ink.

2. Don't know what to say? Get straight to the point, and specifically name the gift or favor. "Thank you so much for the green coffee

mug" or "Thank you very much for the time you took to interview me yesterday" are good starters. Then say how you plan to use the gift, how much you learned during the interview, or something similar. If appropriate, relate a personal anecdote such as, "I just broke my favorite coffee mug" or "I have always wanted to work for a company like this." End with a final thank-you and suitable closing, such as "Best wishes" or "Yours truly."

3. If you didn't like the gift or the meal and you don't think you'd like to work for this particular company, write a thank-you note anyway. Remember, the person spent time and effort on you.

4. Write a note immediately or at least within two weeks. Otherwise, the person my wonder whether you received or liked the gift; an interviewer may forget you altogether.

Tips for Gift Giving
Gifts to clients and prospective clients are a well-established business tradition that can yield long-lasting positive results. But because the practice of giving can be tricky, many industries and individual firms have established rules and guidelines to prevent missteps and backfires. Here are a few general suggestions:

1. Before you give a gift, find out what the gift policy and limit on the gift value are at the company where the recipient works. If individual gifts are frowned on or even prohibited because management fears undue influence, you might still make a

group gift, make a charitable contribution in the company's name, or contribute to a gift matching program.

2. Avoid giving gifts when negotiating or bidding for new business.

3. Give only to those you know well; otherwise, the gesture may backfire.

4. Present the gift with taste and care. Wrap it or have it wrapped and include a handwritten note.

5. If possible, deliver the gift yourself – in person.

6. Be creative about when you give. In addition to traditional gift-giving holidays, consider the date of contract renewal or the anniversary of a business relationship. Or give to commemorate a joint achievement or to celebrate a client's promotion.

7. Be thoughtful and choose a practical gift that you're sure will be appreciated. Know your recipient's taste and interests (sports, hobbies, food, or music preferences) and choose accordingly.

8. Avoid giving a gift that makes the recipient uncomfortable for any reason – steer clear of a gift that is too large, too small, inappropriate, poorly timed, humorous, or too personal.

9. Use restraint. Giving too many gifts reduces their effect and can embarrass the recipient.

10. Recognize that gifts with your company's logo on them may be seen as tacky or impersonal. If you must include it, use the logo in the wrapping and not the gift.

Mastering the Art of Small Talk

As a banker in my other life, when I sat down with a customer to discuss the very personal topic of their money, it was important to make them feel comfortable. It was up to me to offer the personal warmth that creates trust, and that begins with the art of small talk.

Here are a few tips for establishing common ground with a few minutes of polite conversation before getting to the business reason for a meeting.

- Always greet clients by looking them in the eye, smiling, saying their name, and offering a firm handshake and a chair.
- Eliminate any possible distractions such as phone calls or music playing in the office.
- Offer tea, coffee, or other refreshments, if available.
- You can never go wrong by asking, "How are you today?"
- If asked how you are, always respond briefly and turn the conversation back to your customer. Avoid saying anything about being ill or having any personal problems.
- If you are already acquainted with the customer and his or her family, inquire about other family members. You might want to keep a brief file of personal information about

your regular customers for this purpose. If not, ask whether they have any family, how many, where they live, and so on.

- Remember that people are nearly always eager to talk about their children and grandchildren.
- Even more, people like to talk about themselves – "P2P!" Sometimes all they need is an opening such as a question about their work, their interests and hobbies, recent travels, and so on.
- Borrow a trick from Eleanor Roosevelt, who would mentally run through the alphabet thinking of topics to introduce in conversation. For instance, "A" might remind you of animals, and you can ask whether a person has any pets; "B" might suggest books, and you can inquire whether the person has read a popular best-seller; "C" could suggest cuisine, as in, "Have you tried the new restaurant around the corner?"
- Know when to stop. Use observation and empathy to help you determine when the person has started to relax and feel comfortable. Then it's time to ask, "How may I help you today?"

Global Etiquette

Learning About Global Differences

Committing a social blunder at school or at home is one thing, but committing one in a foreign country may mean the end of your business relationship with your host. Each culture has its own set of rules and customs, and before you head out to dinner with your foreign business associates or venture into their country for a meeting, you'll need to learn all you can about global etiquette and what is and is not appropriate abroad.

For instance, in Iraq you shake hands gently, always with the right hand, and do not use your left hand to eat, gesture, or touch others. If a woman is present, allow her to greet you first. She will shake hands with only her fingertips.

Here are some additional little-known facts about other countries and their customs:

1. In Chile, business gifts should be of good quality but not lavish, and women should not give gifts to men because the gesture can be misunderstood.

2. When in South Africa, dress well in public because your host will expect it.

3. In Iraq, if you must point at something, use your entire hand, not just one finger, which is considered a sign of contempt.

4. The Chinese do not speak with their hands, so do not use large gestures and remember that men should not touch women in public.

5. In Egypt, members of the same sex stand much closer to each other than North American and Europeans do, but men and women stand farther apart.

6. Avoid casual dress when doing business in Japan and dress to impress. Remember, shoes will be taken off frequently so they should be easy to remove.

7. It is impolite to show the soles of your shoes in Russia.

8. In Germany, sudden changes in business transactions are unwelcome even if they are positive, and humor in business settings is not encouraged.

Most importantly, learn the basic vocabulary and historical background of the country and region, as well as the proper use of greetings and introductions.

Pay attention to your physical gestures, facial expressions, dress, and dining and drinking habits. Mastering the details can save you embarrassment and perhaps make or break your career.

A Positive Workplace
Means Business!
It Just Makes Cent$! TM

Chapter Thirteen

The Real World

People-to-People ("P2P") Connections
Are Working!

As I see it, a positive workplace means making the people-to-people ("P2P") connections that foster diversity and inclusion of all kinds of people – it's the right, legal, and profitable thing to do! Any organization that continues to see itself as homogeneous is missing the point! Diversity is not limited to differences we can see, in gender, race, and ethnicity. In reality, diversity includes those differences in age, religious affiliation, thinking, styles, physical appearance, abilities, education, and sexual orientation, to name a few.

The winning organizations of the future understand the bottom-line value of attracting and retaining the right people for the right jobs. Organizational leaders that truly support and manage diversity programs and practice inclusion with employees, customers, vendors and shareholders, will rise to the top and emerge as some of the finest 21st century leaders. They will make a *positive impact* on their organization's overall performance, profitability, and market share and will set the tone and example for those who are fortunate enough to learn from them and perpetuate the cycle.

Let's take a look at two well-known companies…

L'Oréal Dedicated to Diversity

In 2004, L'Oréal USA became the first recipient of the Diversity Best Practices' Global Leadership Award. Criteria to receive the award include creating an environment of inclusion and diversity through corporate diversity initiatives, chairing and supporting diversity councils, recognizing community, philanthropic and supplier diversity, and ensuring support of all levels throughout the company.

In addition, L'Oreal's diversity efforts have been recognized by several other international awards:
• 2005: The Anti-Defamation League's International Leadership Award
• 2006: The World Diversity Leadership Council's Diversity Innovation Award
• 2007: L'Oreal ranked as one of the "World's Most Ethical Companies" according to Ethisphere Magazine.

L'Oréal's chief diversity officer, Jean Paul Agon, tracks, monitors and benchmarks the progress of the company's U.S. diversity programs. Under his guidance, L'Oréal's ambition is to:
• reflect, in its teams and at every level, the diversity of its clients (in terms of nationality, ethnic or social origin, age...), coherently with its employment pools,
• promote the access of women to high-responsibility position and a better gender equity in jobs,
• promote work for disabled people,
• accumulate skills and capitalize on the experience of its employees, taking advantage of the cultural diversity of its teams, extending careers and making use of experience.

Diversity Training for Managers
Since the end of 2006, a specific diversity training program is being rolled-out to 8000 managers in Europe (over 32 countries). This training aims to involve, give responsibility to and help managers in implementing the Group's diversity policy. This training at European level joins the training that has been underway in the USA for two years where more than 2000 have already been trained.

Diversity and Social Cohesion Observatories
Since 2006, 23 Diversity and Social Cohesion Observatories have been set up in France. They are comprised of staff representatives, members of the personnel department and volunteer employees. Their objective is to promote respect for diversity and non-discrimination in the field, implement initiatives and follow-up on them. The group process involves meeting to share information regarding the measures implemented to fight all forms of discrimination, to promote diversity and equity. The implementation of Observatories on an international level has already begun in various European countries.

Some Results
At L'Oreal, at international level, 54% of managers are women. They account for 34% of the members of the management committees. 53% of managers promoted in 2006 were women.
In the Group, there are 112 different nationalities and 60% non-French people are members of the management committee.
In the USA in 2005, minorities represented 19.8% of all managers and 33% of all employees. In South Africa, 51% of managers are "PDI" (Previously Disadvantaged Individuals).

Getting Results from Diversity Training: In Dollars and Cent$

Measuring the effectiveness of training on diversity practices can be difficult. However, a few years ago, Nextel Communications Inc. (now Sprint Nextel) effectively considered the return on investment for training that had traditionally been considered "intangible" in the context of human resource measurement.

The organization developed diversity training for the specific business goal of improving employee retention, satisfaction and productivity through increased diversity awareness. All 13,000 employees took the diversity course. To measure training results, the company created training scorecards. Specifically, the training team determined what would be measured and evaluated, when, how and why. Every participant was provided with the objective of the program and what needed to be accomplished, including checklists of what to do after the diversity class. The training team tracked retention figures for a specific time frame and asked survey participants what percentage of increased retention results they attributed to the training as well as to other variables.

Based on those survey results, the overall decrease in turnover was determined to be 2%, with the training contributing 10% to the change, thus directly retaining 36 people. Turnover costs at the time averaged $89,000 per employee. By multiplying $89,000 by 36 (retained employees), it was determined that the diversity training saved the organization $3,204,000. The conservative calculation of the program cost was $1,216,836, including design development costs, time spent developing the evaluation and time for participants to complete the survey. Thus, the net program benefits divided by the program costs and multiplied by 100 revealed an ROI of 163%. That is, for every dollar spent on diversity training, the company had a $1.63 net benefit.

Fortune Magazine's 100 Best Companies to Work For

We've been reading Fortune Magazine's "Best Companies to Work For" list for many years and we've come to know many of the winners for their popular brand, fine service and reliable products. It's quite a process to apply for consideration.

To pick the 100 Best Companies to Work for, Fortune partners with Great Place to Work Institute® to conduct the most extensive employee survey in corporate America. Of some 1,500 firms that were contacted, 407 companies participated in this year's survey. Nearly 100,000 employees at those companies responded to a 57-question survey created by the Great Place to Work Institute®, a global research and consulting firm with offices in 30 countries.

Most of the company's score (two-thirds) is based on the results of the survey, which is sent to a minimum of 400 randomly selected employees from each company. The survey asks questions related to their attitudes about the management's credibility, job satisfaction and camaraderie. The other third of the scoring is based on the company's responses to the Institute's Culture Audit, which includes detailed questions about demographic makeup, and pay and benefit programs, as well as a series of open-ended questions about the company's management philosophy, methods of internal communications, opportunities, compensation practices, and diversity efforts, etc.

After their evaluations are completed, if news about a company comes to light that may significantly damage employees' faith in management, they may exclude that company from the list.

Any company that is at least seven years old with more than 1,000 U.S. employees is eligible. For an online nomination form, go to www.greatplacetowork.com.

What about the possibility of working for one of these star organizations? Here's what Fortune senior writer, Anne Fisher, had to say in a January 22, 2008 article...

Even during economic downturns, Fortune's 100 Best Companies to Work For are constantly scouting for talent. Here's how to get your foot in the door.

(Fortune Magazine) -- It helps to know someone. Almost all of the 100 Best rely heavily on employee referrals. Principal Financial Group and many others get about 40% of their new hires this way. At Wegmans it's a family thing: About one in five employees are related to at least one other staffer.

Play up volunteer work on your résumé. These companies are enthusiastic about community outreach, and they prefer to hire people who are too.

Get ready to interview and interview... and interview. The process varies wildly from one company to another, but you could be facing a series of 12 to 15 one-on-one chats or one long interview with a panel of up to 50 current employees.

Unleash your inner storyteller. By far the most popular interview style is what's known as behavioral, meaning that you will be asked to describe troublesome situations in past jobs and tell exactly how you handled them.

Do creative research. A proven way to stand out from the hordes of other candidates is to know more about the place and the industry than your rivals. A Google search won't do it. Says Jay Jones, recruiting manager at Alcon Laboratories: "Detailed research, including talking to our customers, is so rare it will almost guarantee you get hired."

No lone rangers need apply. By and large, the 100 Best want team players. "I actually count the number of times a candidate says 'I' in an interview," says Adobe's recruiting director Jeff Vijungco. "We'd much rather hear 'we.'"

If you've moved around a lot, be ready to explain why. A checkered past won't disqualify you, but most of these companies are looking for people who want to build a career over the long haul. Be persuasive about why you're ready to settle down here.

Be open to learning new things. Showing passion is a must, and most of the 100 Best pride themselves on creating "learning environments," so talk about the skills you'd like to acquire or polish. A turnoff: declaring that you're already the best at what you do.

If at first you don't succeed, don't give up. Almost every Best Company keeps track of what FedEx calls "silver medalists" - people who barely missed getting hired - and alerts them to new openings. If possible, register on the company's website. Four Seasons, for one, has hired people seven or eight years after an initial meeting.

Don't coast on their reputation. One final tip: Don't apply for a job just because the company is on our list. In the words of Mike Gallagher, HR director at SAS Institute, "We know we have a reputation as a great place to work. But if the reason you want to work here is that you want subsidized day care or a great gym, you won't last." Or, for that matter, make it through the first round of interviews.

A Positive Workplace Means Business! It Just Makes Cent$! TM

Chapter Fourteen

Closer to Home

People-to-People ("P2P") Connections Are Working

Right here in Connecticut we have two of Fortune's 2008 best companies!

26 Stew Leonard's, Norwalk, CT
(seventh straight year on the list)

49 Griffin Hospital, Derby, CT
(ninth straight year on the list)

Over the past several months, I had the good fortune of sitting down to talk with Jill Leonard Tavello and Patrick Charmel, leaders of these winning organizations, along with the leaders of three other Connecticut businesses and organizations who, I believe, have made a "positive workplace" difference closer to home.

Cindi Bigelow, President, R.C. Bigelow Inc., Fairfield, CT

Larry Janesky, President, Basement Systems Inc., Seymour, CT

Robert D. Scinto, Chairman, R.D. Scinto Inc., Shelton, CT

What a wonderful learning opportunity! I posed the following five questions to them which focused on the people-to-people ("P2P") and diversity aspects of their leadership:

1. What is your personal diversity philosophy? Where/how did it start?

2. What was your "Aha!" moment?

3. When did find out the exact moment you realized diversity was your company's future and essential to your own personal development?

4. What have you done to convey that message to your employees? Vendors? Shareholders?

5. How does your approach and diversity business strategy affect your bottom-line results?

As I pondered over my interview notes and began to create the text for this chapter, I thought about the common threads that ran among each of these leaders. Many of the leadership qualities, characteristics and traits we read or hear about were apparent in these conversations or were easy to trace from the stories told. Positive attitude, courage, humility, hard work from the bottom-up, risk taking, service to others, fair-play, continuous learning, the importance of being a team player, family values, and the willingness to challenge themselves – a healthy discontent.

I'd like to share those discussions and some of their comments with you...

Cindi Bigelow, President,
R.C. Bigelow Inc., Fairfield, CT

Cindi has been working in her family's business for over 22 years. She is loaded with positive energy and learned the business from the bottom up from her parents, David and Eunice Bigelow. Part of the company success is based on Cindi's philosophy that "One of anything is not good. There is great value in different thought processes." She learned over the years that there will always be problem areas in the business and she also learned early on to appreciate the power of a team to help her solve these problems." She says, "It's important to really listen to people and truly see the benefit in what they say." That means putting the best people possible on your team. Part of this entails interviewing for the best fit for each department in which you are hiring.

As President, Cindi mirrors the leadership characteristics she expects of her managers and employees. She works diligently to set a positive work environment, emphasize people's strengths, honor those who work with her and tries to demonstrate every day how much she wants to be doing what she does. "It has to come across in everything you do!" Cindi says. "It is also essential to realize that when challenging issues arise, it's how you work them out - with employees, customers and vendors - that truly shows people your skill sets and character. Strong partnerships are formed through fair play, respect, and hard work."

For over 63 years, the R.C. Bigelow has changed the way we drink tea in the United States. A privately-held company with over 300 employees with locations in Connecticut, Kentucky and Idaho, the little tea company started by Ruth Campbell Bigelow in her family kitchen so many years ago, sold over 1.5 billion cups of tea this past year.

To quote Cindi Bigelow, "Do the right thing and good things will follow..."

Patrick Charmel, President and CEO, Griffin Hospital, Derby, CT

Patrick Charmel has been associated with Griffin Health Services Corporation since 1979 when he became a student intern while attending Quinnipiac College, where he received his bachelor's degree. He received a Masters in Public Health from Yale University and began his career journey as a junior executive, assistant to the president of Griffin Hospital.

Patrick is active in the community he serves and sits on several boards of directors, one being the Greater Valley Chamber of Commerce, which is where we first met in December 2006. As chair of an upcoming fundraising event, I sought Patrick out after that meeting to solicit his help...without hesitation, he agreed to help me.

When I contacted him regarding an interview for this book, again, without hesitation, he agreed. I thought how fortunate it would be to have thirty minutes of this busy man's time; as it turned out, we had quite a wonderful conversation for more than one hour. This, again, spoke volumes to me about Patrick's giving nature and his rise to success.

I asked him about his first job and what lessons he took away from it. He laughed as he told me…"I started working at 15 years old at a Hess gas station in my home state of New Jersey. There were no self-service stations then, nor are there any today, so a customer service orientation was instilled in me at an early age. Hess held the gold standard for service; we had to pay close attention to detail by checking the oil, the tires, cleaning windshields, etc. I gave good service and even had fun with the customers, who in turn gave me good tips!"

We then talked about diversity and the "people-to-people" connections and Patrick talked quite a bit about the importance of recognizing differences as strengths. He realized in his early 20's when there was not a lot of diversity, that it was not only the right thing to do but, had great benefits for all involved. "We feel it's important to develop a team of caregivers who value relationships, have complimentary skills and, most importantly, who have the right attitude." People with different strengths and talents place more than 7500 applications for work each year at Griffin for only 150 open jobs. Patrick's "hire for attitude" philosophy is critical in the stressful healthcare environment where high expectations and outcomes prevail.

Patrick explained that he spends quite a bit of time talking to employees, vendors, volunteers, and those in the community about the Planetree philosophy - hospital care that is humanistic and more responsive and empowering to consumers so they can be involved in their care. It is a patient-centered, healing environment with a name that evolved from

Hipocrates, who taught students under the planetree, and means "transfer knowledge."

During the first six months of employment, employees learn about the hospital's philosophy and their role in the organization's success. New hires participate in a five-day orientation that includes a two-day/overnight retreat in an austere conference center that is a former convent where caregivers are taught what it is like to be a patient. They feed each other, serve each other and experience what it is like to rely on someone else for help. In addition, they spend two and one half hours with Patrick where he talks about the service culture and relationship building. "We stress the importance of building positive working relationships," he says. "It's a big investment; we want them to be successful. Customer expectations are high; lives are on the line."

The hospital also provides the opportunity for employees to develop personally through the decade old "Dare to Care" program, which teaches tools and techniques about dealing with life, such as goal setting, perseverance, and courage. It is truly a "people-to-people" connection since the programs are taught by many of the 300+ graduates of the program. "It is our gift to our employees," says Patrick. He goes on to say, "Employees and potential employees at all levels must be willing to spend the time to build productive relationships in the workplace. It's all about employee pride – pride in product, in team, in leaders and in the service. When employees see the visitors from all over the world, it reinforces Planetree all over. The employee pride and resulting retention speaks for itself." This is an organization of high standards and achievers and it is apparent to me that Patrick both talks the talk and walks the walk.

Charmel has positioned Griffin Hospital as an award-winning, innovative organization outperforming peer organizations by developing and implementing consumer-driven, patient-focused services that result in high patient satisfaction, while maintaining high operational efficiency. Fundamental to Griffin's philosophy is empowering people and providing the knowledge to make them active partners responsible for maintaining their health and making decisions about their care and treatment. Griffin is committed to listening to patients and the public, developing and offering services, programs and care which focus on prevention and wellness, and to providing quality medical care.

Griffin was featured in *Inc. Magazine*, on CBS This Morning, CNBC, *The Wall Street Journal*, *Healthy Body, Healthy Mind* Series on PBS, in Tom Peter's *On Achieving Excellence* newsletter, *Prevention Magazine*, *The Healthcare Forum Journal* and numerous American Hospital Association, and hospital industry publications.

Most recently, Griffin Hospital celebrated its ninth year on Fortune Magazine's "100 Best Companies to Work for in America" list. Griffin was ranked 4th in 2006, its highest position yet, up from 8th overall the year before. Griffin is the only hospital in the country named to the list nine years in a row. It joins such nationally recognized companies as Microsoft, Nordstroms, Four Seasons Hotels and the Mayo Clinic. Griffin has been the smallest company on the list in terms of revenue, and ranked #1 among small companies in 2006.

In Search Of Excellence author Tom Peters said: "Griffin Hospital has earned widespread recognition, increased staff and patient satisfaction and bragging rights as the best healthcare environment in the country." The most important part of the quote is "increased patient satisfaction." Patients now give Griffin Hospital's care the highest ratings in their history.

Spending time with Patrick helped me to better understand Griffin's commitment and passion for providing a new wellness, prevention health model with consumer-driven services and care.

Patrick Charmel is truly leadership-in-action with the vision of making the community a better place in which to live, work, raise a family and enjoy life.

In his own words, "We must be with the people – the customers and employees – work hard to earn their trust and hold ourselves accountable as leaders."

Larry Janesky, President, Basement Systems Inc., Seymour, CT

"Everything flows from the leaders; put emotions aside, use logic." This is a quote from Larry about his personal business philosophy. Basement Systems is the world leader in developing and providing products that result in dry, below-grade space. The company has a network of more than 300 dealers throughout the United States, Canada, the United Kingdom, and Ireland.

Visiting the corporate offices of Basement Systems is truly a treat. From the history wall that begins with Larry's original tool belt noting his start in the construction industry to the 1950's soda shop motif of the company cafeteria, the positive workplace environment is apparent. Employees seem happy working in their open floor plan environment. Larry sets the tone with his open style, positive can-do attitude, and overall, "nice guy" presence.

His business and corporate culture philosophy is simple…"A company needs to relate to its customers; employees are the company and can relate to the customers if they are different. We hire the best person for the job, no matter what. Many employees start at the bottom as I did and move up in the organization by finding what the customer values in greater quality or quantity."

Larry says as the owner of a growing business today, he needs to continually look at what workforce is available to do the work and serve the customer. "At Basement Systems, we hire for attitude, nice people from every walk of life, with a good work ethic. Hire those who appreciate it all, exceed their expectations and they will remain good, loyal employees."

Larry is quick to tell you that he doesn't like turnover or unfairness and gossip and his actions speak as loud as his words. He says it's important to "know yourself and make up your personal gaps with hiring choices. I try to step out of my comfort zone and hire those that are not like me – step out of my personal box. Not about group think – an organization will get stuck if group think prevails."

Robert D. Scinto, Chairman,
R. D. Scinto, Inc., Shelton, CT

A recent area newspaper article's business page headline read, "Optimism Breeds Optimism," quite a change from most other headlines these days. As I began to read the article, I understood why it was different. It involved Robert D. Scinto, Chairman of R. D. Scinto, Inc., Shelton, CT.

Bob, as he is known in the business community, has, quite deservedly, become a nearly legendary figure as a man who embodies the best of America's Dream of the self-made man. He has risen from night school and the successful rehabilitation of a three-family house to owning approximately 2.9 million square feet of office and industrial buildings in Fairfield County. Bob Scinto has constructed, owns and manages all of his buildings. His portfolio is always occupied, well in excess of industry averages. The company that began in the basement of a Bridgeport housing project is now a $500 million organization.

A few months ago, I sat in the reception area of "Corporate Towers One" eagerly anticipating my meeting with Bob. After a short wait, he arrived and escorted me to his office. There began my journey with him. I sat along side his desk and offered to step out of the room as he accepted several unscreened phone calls, "not necessary," he said. I was fascinated and in awe while watching this successful man in action. I became absorbed in the professional, yet, open, positive feel of my comfortable natural wood surroundings. From the glass door entry, extensive collection of books, loads of family pictures, the Broadway music playing in the background to the many inspirational and spiritual reminders on the walls and in the bookcases. Two wall plaques that spoke volumes about Bob's philosophy of life were hung nearby: "Nothing is impossible." and "It can be done." The puzzle pieces were coming together…This man of lofty stature with a wide sparkling smile was as authentic and genuine as I could ever have imagined.

In between calls and being called out to issues that needed his immediate attention, we talked at length about his humble beginnings. I asked about when he first realized that diversity and service were important to his company's future and essential to personal development. Bob responded, "It was early on as a plumber when doing a job for a welfare mother. She was so appreciative and humbly thanked Jesus for sending her the plumber! It was then I knew that the number one concept for my company would be 'service.'"

To this day, he sets the example and a high standard for his employees. "If you treat employees with dignity, respect and kindness, they will treat customers and tenants the same way. Retention, reputation, the way you treat everyone – It's everything in business!"

A well-read, self-made man, Bob said he continues to do quite a bit of reading and, in his opinion, "there are three essential books to read and the only ones you'll ever need: *The Road Less Traveled, 7 Habits of Highly Effective People*, and *How to Win Friends and Influence People."*

A man who watches details, Bob Scinto graces his buildings with sculptures and aesthetic touches that are much more than trim but confirm his concern for quality. His innovative inclusion of day-care facilities in some of his projects underscores his willingness to get out in front when he believes something is important. A man with a strong sense of place and natural rapport and respect for people, Bob Scinto is a man for the long-term.

His outstanding success in real estate is, in part, the result of his total commitment to his work and his considerable abilities. It is also the result of a levelheaded management style, a well-deserved reputation for integrity and for staying close to the demands of his tenants, industry, and community.

During his business career, he has served the greater community by actively participating on 15 boards and he is most fond of those organizations that directly benefit ordinary people.

I am honored to know Bob Scinto and grateful for the opportunity to visit with him. He gets it – It's all about attitude and the people-to-people connections!

Bob's enthusiasm, personal loyalty and genuine concern for all human beings motivates his employees, befriends his tenants and earns the respect and fear of his competition. His personal mission statement would best be described in the words of George Bernard Shaw:

"I am of the opinion that my life belongs to the whole community and as long as I live it is my privilege to do for it whatever I can. I want to be thoroughly used up when I die. For the harder I work the more I live. I rejoice in life for its own sake. Life is no brief candle to me. It's a sort of splendid torch which I've got to hold up for the moment and I want to make it burn as brightly as possible before handing it on to future generations."

Optimism breeds optimism...

Jill Leonard Tavello, Vice President Culture and Communication, Stew Leonard's, Norwalk, CT

A recent article in the *Fairfield County Business Times,* titled, "A Fresh Approach Drives Success," began with the following paragraph:

Amid the gloomy economic forecast that is dominating business news these days, it is a refreshing change of pace to recognize companies that strive to maintain an upbeat atmosphere and positive culture. Norwalk-based Stew Leonard's had repeatedly proven itself in this respect.

Since the early 1920's, Stew Leonard's has enjoyed a long and successful history in Fairfield County, CT. Charles Leo Leonard founded Clover Farms Dairy in Norwalk, offering fresh milk delivered daily by trucks with plastic cows on the front that mooed for neighborhood children.

As progress brings change, in the late 1960's, Charles' son, Stew, who ran Clover Farms from the time he turned 21, founded a small dairy store in 1969 with seven employees and carrying just eight items. His dream of building a retail dairy store where children could watch milk being bottled while mothers did their shopping in a farmer's market atmosphere came alive. Stew Leonard's has grown to become one of the most renowned grocery stores in the region. With over 2000 team members in their Connecticut and New York locations, Stew Leonard's founding principles of quality and service remain unchanged.

Jill Leonard Tavello, as many successful people have, started at the bottom – as a cashier over 30 years ago. She said, "Being right with the customers is where I learned how important it was to talk with the customer. I had to introduce myself, find out their name, what they were buying and make small talk. It's all about making connections to the people – providing the products and services for what the customer wants at the time." From the moment we began our conversation, I knew Jill really lived and believed in this philosophy.

Stew Leonard realized that learning about the people was a critical component in creating a successful business and instilled his philosophy of "happy people make happy customers" in his children and employees. Jill said, "My Dad had a helping nature and a very positive attitude. He always tried to give what he could to make team members feel that they were part of the family. If we take care of the people, they will take care of customers." That philosophy has grown to be the brand of the Stew Leonard's culture.

Along with its friendly, casual atmosphere, Stew Leonard's approach to customer service can be summed up with its two rules: Rule #1 – The customer is always right. Rule #2 – If the customer is ever wrong, re-read rule #1. This principle is etched in a three-ton granite rock at each store's entrance!

Jill and her family attribute the success of their venture to passion. In Jill's words, "My father always emphasized how important it is to care about the people. We really care about our team members here and as a result, the team members really take care of the customer."

Speaking about recognition, for the seventh year in a row, *Fortune* magazine has named Stew Leonard's one of the "100 Best Companies to Work For." They ranked 26th on the prestigious list, and are one of only three Connecticut-based companies chosen.

As Vice President of Culture and Communication, one of Jill's responsibilities include the *Fortune* application each year. "We go through a microscope and are rated on five principles – credibility, fairness, respect, pride and camaraderie. Two thirds of the company's score for the *Fortune* ranking is based on the results of an employee survey, which is sent to 400 randomly selected employees. When we receive our survey results, we communicate them to our team members and seize the opportunities for improvement and make constructive changes."

In *Fortune's* words, "Known for its rah-rah culture, this supermarket chain opened its fourth store in Newington, Conn., creating 430 new jobs (85 percent of managers were hired in-house)." The magazine notes that Stew Leonard's had a 13 percent job growth in the past year, and nearly half of its workforce is composed of minorities and women. Aside from statistics, Tavello says, "Having happy team members means our customers will have a great experience when they come to our stores."

Managing growth and communication are challenges in most organizations and Stew Leonard's is no different. "With so many generations in the workforce today and the increased use of technology, leaders are expected to communicate in so many more ways that before. As Dean of Stew's University, we continue to focus on developing the people skills in our team members and the importance of being able to communicate with all levels of people." says Jill. She went on to say, "We believe in developing our team members. Another tangible benefit to being on the *Fortune* list is to attract and retain top talent. When we opened our new store in Newington, we received more than 3,000 applications for the 350 available positions, largely based on our reputation as a great place to work. Most of our managers and leaders have started on the front lines and worked their way up; close to ninety percent have been promoted from within."

Some of the ways Jill has found to be effective motivation and communication vehicles:
- Daily team member newsletter noting birthdays, special events, success stories
- Monthly focus group lunches with the store president and Jill to hear from front line team members
- "Sweaty Palm Award" – for team members stepping outside their comfort zone
- "Ladders of Success" recognition program promoting careers
- "Mom's Program" - Flexible work schedules to help them with work/life balance

Stew Leonard's proven tradition of team member and customer satisfaction will guarantee continued success as the business continues to grow. "As we grow, we don't want to become a 'chain' or have 'chain mentality," says Jill. "We all really love what we do and will keep the message growing. We hire the people that have a great attitude and the necessary skills; as my brother, Stew Jr., says, 'we work with great people who are passionate about what they do, who like to put effort into it because they do love it and because it's fun.'"

A Positive Workplace Means Business! It Just Makes Cent$! TM

Chapter Fifteen

Turn Up Your "Dimmer Switch!"
Make a Positive Impact on Bottom-Line Results!

✓ **Want to spend less money on recruiting employees?**
✓ **Want to reduce turnover?**
✓ **Want to increase productivity by 35%?**
✓ **Did you know it costs about 250% of salary (recruiting, training, operational time) each time an employee turns over?**

The Road to Results is Through Your Employees!

Reduce Costly Turnover by Understanding The Real Reasons Why Employees Look for New Jobs!

Top Seven Reasons
1. The job or workplace is not as expected.
2. The person did not match the job.
3. Too little coaching and feedback early on.
4. Too few growth opportunities.
5. Stress from over work.
6. Loss of trust and confidence in leaders.
7. Not being recognized or feeling valued.

Positive Solutions

1. Manager's attitude sets the tone – *Stay Positive!*
2. Implement a behavioral-based interviewing system.
3. Effective time management; make the time for your people.
4. Cross-training, projects, volunteer work.
5. Balance the work, make healthy lifestyle choices, have more fun!
6. Be a role model – Walk the walk, talk the talk! Leadership training
7. Demonstrate workplace courtesy; improve reward and recognition programs.

A Positive Workplace
Means Business!
It Just Makes Cent$! TM

Resources and References

Bayer,Lewana and Mallett, Karen, "Telephone Etiquette," accessed August 15, 2005, Lifewise, http://www.canoe.ca

Bly, Laura, "The Tipping Point," *USA Today*, August 26, 2005, p. 1D; "Tipping Etiquette: Travel," All Sands.com, accessed May 4, 2005, http://www.allsands.com

Boone and Kurtz. Contemporary Business 2006, Cincinnati, Ohio, Thomson Southwestern, 2006.

Bremer, Jill, "Cubicle Etiquette," Bremer Communications, accessed June 7, 2006, http://www.bremercommunications.com; "Cubicle Culture Isn't Necessarily Very Private," accessed June 7, 2006, http://www.herald-dispatch.com

Bureau of Labor Statistics, "Most Common Uses for Computers at Work," U.S. Department of Labor, accessed July 21, 2006, http://www.bls.gov

The Business Case For Diversity. (2001). Allegiant Media. Retrieved February 10, 2002 from http://www.diversityinc.com/articles.

"Business Etiquette," Newspaper Association of America, accessed June 27, 2006, http://www.naa.org

Chapman, Elwood, McKnight, Wil, Attitude: Your Most Priceless Possession, Boston, MA, Thomson Publishing, 2002.

Conference Board, www.conferenceboard.org, accessed 2003.

Cox, Taylor, Jr., (1993). Cultural Diversity in Organizations. San Francisco: Berrett-Koehler, p. 11, 169-170, 261.

Demographic Information. Retrieved January 24, 2002, from http://diversitydtg.com/articles/demographics

Demographic Information (2001). Retrieved February 9, 2002, from http://www.census.gov/demographics

Diversity Is a Priority, www.loreal.com, Our Company, Our Teams; retrieved December 13, 2008.

Edidin, Peter, "How to Shake Hands or Share a Meal with an Iraqi," *The New York Times*, March 6, 2005, p. WK 7; "City Tips," *Worth*, March 2005

"Email Etiquette," Online Writing Lab at Purdue University, accessed July 20, 2006, http://owl.english.purdue.edu

"Email Etiquette," AllBusiness, accessed July 20, 2006, http://www.allbusiness.com

Gamonal, Paula, "Doing Business in Europe,"*Ravenwerks*, accessed July 15, 2006, http://www.ravenwerks.com

Gardenswartz, L. & Rowe, A., (1998). Managing Diversity: A Complete Desk Reference and Planning Guide. Chicago: McGraw Hill.

Gardenswartz, L. & Rowe, A., (1998). *Why Diversity Matters*, HR Focus, p.75.

Gates, Stephen, *Measuring More Than Efficiency: The New Role of Human Capital Metrics,* The Conference Board, Report 1356-04-RR, 2004, Retrieved June 7, 2007.

"Gift Giving Etiquette," American Express, accessed August 16, 2006, http://www.133.americanexpress.com

Grove, Cornelius & Associates, (1995, 2002). *Diversity in Business, What it is. Why it's useful. How it works,* Retrieved June 7, 2007, from www.shrm.org/resources

"Harness E-Mail: E-Mail Etiquette," Learn the Net, accessed July 20, 2006, http://learnthenet.com

Harpold, Leslie, "How to Write a Thank-you Note," *The Morning News,* accessed July 12, 2006, http://www.themorningnews.org

Harvard Business School Press, http://www.hbsp.harvard.edu, accessed 2003.

Hastings, Rebecca R., SPHR, *SHRM Research Shows Diversity Making Progress*, (2006). Retrieved June 7, 2007, from www.shrm.org/resources.

Hetherington, Mike, "Client Gifts That Keep On Giving," *Bozeman (MT) Daily Chronicle,* accessed July 21, 2006, http://www.bozemandailychronicle.com

Higuera,Valencia P., "Techniques to Remember Names," FineTuning.com, accessed July 25, 2005, http://www.finetuning.com

Ho, Mimi, "Internet Surfing at the Workplace," *CIO*, accessed July 21, 2006, http://www.2.cio.com

"Holiday Etiquette," Eticon, accessed July 21, 2006, http://www.eticon.com

"How Do I Remember People's Names?" LearnThat, accessed August 15, 2005, http://www.learnthat.com

"How to Master Small Talk," Canadian Business Online, accessed July 3, 2006, http://canadianbusiness.com

International Business Center Web site, accessed June 11, 2006, http://www.cyborlink.com

Kulman, Linda, "Thank-You-Note Writing 101," *U.S. News & World Report*, May 9, 2005, p. D12

Lang, Bob, "Proper Business Etiquette for Using Electronic Communication Devices," accessed June 27, 2006, http://www.baltimoremd.com

"Learning Small Talk," Mannersmith, accessed August 16, 2006, http://www.mannersmith.com

Lebeau, Mary, "The Fine Art of 'Cube-tiquette,'" JobWeb, accessed June 7, 2006, http://www.jobweb.com

Leonard, Melissa, "Avoid the 'Fatal' Faux pas," ABA Banking Online, accessed July 27, 2006, http://www.ababj.com

Lockwood, Nancy R., (2005). *Measuring Return on Investment for Diversity Management,* Retrieved June 7, 2007, from www.shrm.org/research

Lockwood, Nancy R., (2006). *The Impact of Diversity Initiatives,* Retrieved June 7, 2007, from www.shrm.org/research

Loden, Marilyn, (1996). Implementing Diversity. Boston: McGraw Hill.

Lorenz, Kate, "Tricks to Remembering Names," CNN.com, accessed July 18, 2006, http://www.cnn.com

Marrinan, Michele, "Beware of Wandering Mouse," Monster.com, accessed July 21, 2006, http://www.monster.com

Miller, Frederick A., (Summer 1998). *Strategic Culture Change: The Door to Achieving High Performance and Inclusion.* Public Personnel Management, p. 27.

"Monitoring Employees' Use of Company Computers and the Internet," Texas Workforce, accessed July 21, 2006, http://www.twc.state.tx.us

Morgan, Rebecca L., "Handling Interruptions in a High-Tech Environment," iVillage, accessed June 27, 2006, http://www.ivillage.com.uk

Morrison, Ann M., Ruderman, Marian N., & Hughes-James, Martha. (1993). Making Diversity Happen. Greensboro: The Center for Creative Leadership, p. 3, 19-21.

Mueller, Karen Price, (1998). *Diversity and The Bottom Line,* Harvard Management Update, p. 8-9.

"Peter Post," *Boston Globe,* accessed July 31, 2005, http://www.boston.com

Ramachandran, Nisha, "Office Manners," *U.S. News & World Report,* April 25, 2005, p. EE8.

Ramsey, Lydia, "Sealing the Deal over the Business Meal," *Consulting to Management,* accessed June 17, 2006, http://www.c2m.com

Reeves, Scott, "Hosting a Business Dinner," *Forbes*, accessed June 17, 2006, http://www.forbes.com

Smith, Derek A., (1999). *Leading Diversity: Benchmarking Successful Practices for The Global Market Place.* Linkage Research handout

"Social/Conventional Etiquette," San Jose State University Career Center, accessed July 15, 2006, http://www.sjsu.edu

Survey Report, 2006 Workplace Diversity and Changes to the EEO-1 Process, Retrieved June 7, 2007, www.shrm.org/research/surveys

"Telephone Etiquette," Essortment, accessed July 2, 2006, http://mt.essortment.com

"Telephone Etiquette Guide," California State University, Fullerton: Information Technology, accessed July 2, 2006, http://www.fullerton.edu

"Tipping Etiquette," FindaLink.net, accessed June 8, 2006, http://findalink.net; "Proper Tipping Etiquette," Essortment, accessed June 8, 2006, http://msms.essortment.com

Torre Poulson, Naomi, "Hosting a Formal Dinner," AskmMen.com, accessed June 17, 2006, http://askmen.com

Towers Perrin, *2003 Engagement Survey*, www.towersperrin.com, accessed 2004.

"Travelocity Business Makes Travel Easier with Hints on Tipping," *Business Wire*, accessed June 8, 2006, www.corporate-ir.net

Velasquez, Mauricio, *A Starting Point...Making a Business Case for Diversity.* (2004). Retrieved June 7, 2007 from www.diversitydtg.com/articles

"Web Surfing as Addictive as Coffee," CNN.com, accessed July 21, 2006, http://edition.cnn.com

Weber, Tom, "How to Remember names," The Sideroad, http://www.sideroad.com, accessed August 15, 2005.

Werland, Ross, "Avoid Offending By Learning Foreign Etiquette," Chicago Tribune, www.Vayama.com, accessed summer 2008.

Witt, Susan, "International Business: Learn Your Client's Cultural Sensitivities Before You Travel," WomensMedia.com, http://www.womensmedia.com, accessed July 15, 2006.

Workplace Diversity. (1999). Retrieved February 10, 2002 from http://www.SHRM.org/diversity

Ziglar, Zig. Success for Dummies, Foster City, CA, 1998

A Positive Workplace
Means Business!
It Just Makes Cent$! TM